Norme dueuphal

របស់ ឯកឧត្តម

១០.១០.២០១៨

វិទ្យាស្ថានកម្ពុជា ដើម្បីសន្តិភាពនិងការអភិវឌ្ឍ
Cambodian Institute for Peace and Development (CIPD)

#72 Street 70
Phnom Penh, Cambodia
T: (855-12) 955-858
E: cipdcambodia@gmail.com
W: www.cipdcambodia.org

Norng Chan Phal: The Mystery of the Boy at S-21

Kok-Thay ENG (Ph.D.)

1.   Cambodia—S-21—Survivor Story
2.   Cambodia—Politics and Government—20th Century
3.   Cambodia—Contemporary History—Genocide
4.   Cambodia—Khmer Rouge Regime—1975-1979

The views expressed in this book are the points of view of the author only.

Cover and book concept: Kok-Thay ENG
Graphic design: Sok Kong

Photo Credits: Norng Chan Phal, Kok-Thay ENG

Cover Photo: *1. Norng Chan Phal (not in photo) along with other orphans chanting peace and calling for end of war while receiving a Hungarian delegates in 1986. (photo courtesy of CIPD); 2. Norng Chan Phal in 2012 (photo courtesy of DC-Cam)*

ISBN: 978-99963-900-6-7

Printed in Phnom Penh, Cambodia

ACKNOWLEDGEMENTS

The completion of this book requires hard work, dedication and time. It would not be possible without the following people who have helped me along the way in the forms of encouragement, ideas and information. I am indebted to H.E. Suos Yara, a survivor of the Khmer Rouge genocide, a cultural campaigner and an ardent politician for his encouragement, guidance and material supports in research and publication of the book. Without his backing this book would not have been published. His support allowed Norng Chan Phal's personal journey under the Khmer Rouge to be known to the world.

I am grateful to Huy Vannak, Huot Kheangveng and Mon Ramandy for their moral supports in different ways toward completion of the book. I am thankful to Kosal Phat and Im Sothearith who provided assistance along the way. I would like to thank Chhay Visoth, director of Toul Sleng Genocide Museum, for his assistance in various ways toward completion of this biography. I appreciate information provided by Norng Chan Phal himself, his surviving brothers and Yin Nean.

I am thankful and respectful to Cambodian historians and researchers Youk Chhang, David Chandler, Ben Kiernan, George Chigas, Alexander Hinton, Steve Heder, Frank Chalk, David Hawk, Helen Jarvis, Andrew Rigby, Alan Hunter, Chea Phala and Craig Etcheson whose early and dedicated works contributed greatly to understanding the Khmer Rouge genocide for Cambodia's younger generations. They have contributed over time in different capacities. Their effort allowed peace, reconciliation and forgiveness in Cambodia to take place after genocide. In different fields, they provided valuable guidance, encouragement and academic knowledge without exhaustion not just to me but to other researchers in Cambodian history, politics and Khmer Rouge atrocities.

Lim Ky, deputy director of the national archives, has been greatly helpful. I am delighted for support from Kampot provincial office, the national archives, the national library, ministry of interior, ministry of culture and Tuol Sleng Genocide Museum. I owe the following friends and colleagues for their assistance in varying capacities: Vanthan P. Dara, Dy Khamboly, Som Bunthorn, Nhean Socheat, Chy Terith, Prum Phalla, Long Dany, Kim Sovanndany, Pheng Pong Rasy, Sok Vannak, Meas Bunthan, Sa Fatily, Long Aun, Chheng Veng, Mam Sophat, Sok Kong and Em Chhart.

Abbreviations and Terms

Angkar Padevat:	The leaders of the Communist Party of Kampuchea
ASEAN:	Association of Southeast Asian Nations
CGDK:	Coalition Government of Democratic Kampuchea
CIA:	Central Intelligence Agency
CPK:	Communist Party of Kampuchea
DK:	Democratic Kampuchea
ECCC:	Extraordinary Chambers in the Courts of Cambodia
ICP:	Indochinese Communist Party
KGB:	Komitet Gosudarstvennoi Bezopasnosti (Soviet Secret Police)
KPNLF:	Khmer People's National Liberation Front
KPRC:	Kampuchean People's Revolutionary Council
KPRP:	Khmer People's Revolutionary PartyMovement of the Lost [Misled]: Chalana Samrab Neak Vongveng Phlov
NUFSK:	National United Front for Salvation of Kampuchea
PRK:	People's Republic of Kampuchea
RGC:	Royal Government of Cambodia
SOC:	State of Cambodia
UFCDM:	United Front for the Construction and Defense of the Motherland
UNICEF:	United Nations Children's Fund
UNTAC:	United Nation Transitional Authority in CambodiaVietnamese Volunteer Troops: Kang Toap Smak Chet Vietnam
WFP:	World Food Program

CONTENTS

FOREWORDS

The Khmer Rouge regime led by Saloth Sar held power in Cambodia for three years, eight months and twenty days, from April 17, 1975 to January 6, 1979. During this short period, there were three million people died of execution, forced labors, starvation and diseases. "Khmer Rouge" was a name given to communist groups in Cambodia by Prince Norodom Sihanouk in the 1960s in his Khmerization program which attempts to conflate Cambodia's identity groups into one collective Khmer identity. The prince showed respect for Cambodian people's subordinate identities by appending to the term Khmer a marker that differentiated whether one was a Buddhist, a Muslim, hill tribesman, communist or liberal.

His clearest mention of the term Khmer Rouge occurred in 1967 in relation to the presence and increasing influence of the communists in rural areas of Cambodia. Communism was a popular political movement in the first half of the 20th century. Early communists perceived economic injustice and exploitation of the poor by the rich, of the illiterate by the educated, and of rural farmers by urban dwellers. Such idealism was powerful enough to persuade thousands of young Cambodian to join communist movement. Yet among the communists there were those who were true patriots and those who were delusional and wanted revenge against the country. The delusional group wanted a "modern and progressive" future for Cambodia in which everyone was equal, and there were no crimes, no social classes, no rich, no poor and no diversity. They wanted blood for success of their program. The real patriots wanted salvation for the people.

In their attempt to cleanse the country of perceived impurities, the delusional group created extensive network of security centers and killing fields in which millions of Cambodian were unjustly imprisoned, tortured and executed. One of the most notorious center was S-21. During its existence, up to 14,000 people were incarcerated, brutally tortured and butchered at Cheung Ek killing field several kilometers away. Norng Chan Phal was one of the four children to have survived S-21. This book is first the attempt to lay out his personal story of resilience for the younger generation to learn and put their personal life stories into perspective. As a child Norng Chan Phal suffered tremendously from the loss of his parents at S-21, a happy childhood and the struggle of living as an orphan. The work of the CPP in the past 39 years have changed Cambodia beyond recognition. Unfortunately, progress and development have created an illusion of comfort and a detectable sense of amnesia for the recent dark past. This is why this book is so important for memory, justice and reconciliation.

When we consider the Khmer Rouge period in comparison with the rest of Cambodian history, it is very short. But enough happened under the Khmer Rouge in terms of Khmer identity that this part of history deserves a great attention which is why I continue to support research and understanding of Khmer Rouge genocide for the next generations and to keep reminding my fellow Cambodians that the period in which we are enjoying is hard earned.

There was a time in the depth of war when the idea of peace in the people's mind remained a far fletch imagination. When someone suggested an images of a Cambodia with extensive infrastructure allowing accessibility to all corners of the country, most people would scoff at him as wishful thinker. Such progress is no longer an imagination. The CPP alone has achieved that dream and raised millions of Cambodians from misery, poverty and the ashes of war. I am content that development will continue so long as Khmer people work together in good faith and put the country first in their agendas.

Samdech Akeak Moha Sena Padei Techu Hun Sen has repeatedly stated that without peace there is no development, and secondarily without continuous and gradual development there is no lasting peace. Peace and development has positive correlation as do the relationship between war and destruction. This fact has been true in many parts of the post-conflict world. Peace must be made in the beginning but as it progresses it must be accompanied by sustainable and equitable development for all members of society to truly enjoy the sanctity of social harmony, thereby preventing reversion to war. This is a theory personally envisioned by the Prime Minister, which has paid the way for his many other key policies such as win-win policy in 1998, rectangular strategies and post-conflict reconciliation schemes.

Suos Yara
Member of Parliament

INTRODUCTION

The Khmer Rouge finally gained control of the entire country on April 17, 1975 when Phnom Penh fell in a bloodless final stage of the war. A number of radical plans were then implemented by the Khmer Rouge to keep Cambodians from rebelling and to achieve their grandiose long-term vision of a utopian Cambodia. Phnom Penh and other town centers were evacuated to control the people. Men, women, and children, and even hospital patients and the elderly, were ordered to leave by foot to the countryside. However, the Khmer Rouge did not have a specific plan of how to divide people. They just knew that towns had to be dispersed to the countryside. In Phnom Penh, people chose to walk along major highways to the villages where they used to live or had close relatives. However, because a curfew was imposed, some people could not travel to the village of their choice. Furthermore, they expected to return to Phnom Penh within a few days.

In December 1975, Khmer Rouge leaders and officials met to discuss the creation of a new national Constitution which they passed in January 1976. In the same year Democratic Kampuchea eliminated the old administrative divisions and created new divisions based on zones, regions, districts, communes and villages. They created 6 zones with 32 regions. In 1976, Democratic Kampuchea officials also met to create a four-year plan to be implemented from 1977 to 1980 in which agriculture was the main production priority, to be achieved via collectivization, cooperative units and de-privatization.

The Khmer Rouge's downfall was a result of many factors. Among them: 1) the Khmer Rouge's purge of its own cadres in the Eastern and Central zones and mass killing of the population had forced some of their members to flee to Vietnam and form a resistance force, 2) its own military was weakened due to massacres, lack of effective training and lack of equipment, and 3) nationalists who risked their lives to seek salvation for the people.

The fighting between Democratic Kampuchea and Vietnam started in 1976 and continued throughout 1978 and by the end of the year, Vietnam had mobilized several divisions along its border with Cambodia. In April 1978 Radio Hanoi broadcast messages to encourage Cambodians to continue to defect to Vietnam or rise up to fight against the Khmer Rouge in their villages. It was true that toward the end of 1978, the Khmer Rouge had lost effective control of the purged Eastern Zone. Facing imminent death, many Khmer Rouge cadres either defected to Vietnam or resisted the Khmer Rouge's forces sent from the Southwest Zone and Phnom Penh to capture them. Some did both. Mat Ly was a case in point. He and his communist colleagues escaped the Khmer Rouge massacre and formed a resistance force in the forest before they escaped to Vietnam.

It took the Khmer Rouge a few decades before they began to gain real traction toward power. They first got lucky when Lon Nol staged a coup against Sihanouk in 1970, but then fought for another five years to gain complete control of Cambodia and its symbolic city of Phnom Penh. Then their fate changed again, and the regime fell to the Vietnamese and the Front in less than two weeks. This time, however, it wasn't a turn of luck, but rather a result of the mass killings and starvation that had brought destruction to the regime from within long before the Vietnamese arrived. For the Cham people, the Khmer Rouge's downfall was a blessing, but it came a bit late.

Comrade Hun Sen escaped the Khmer Rouge mass killings on June 21 1977. He had joined the Khmer Rouge to liberate his country from Lon Nol's unjust control and usurpation from a popular Prince Norodom Sihanouk. This time he was seeking salvation for the Khmer people at the hands of Pol Pot and his clique whose main intent was to destroy Cambodia and its people in a delusional belief in rapid change. Along with four of his comrades namely Nuch Than, Nheuk Huon, Sou Kim Sreang (aka Sanh) and Va Pao Eang, Hun Sen succeeded in reaching the safety of Vietnam. The five escapees had met a village called Koh

Thmor in Memot district where they began their dangerous journey without their wife and children through Khmer Rouge controls and an uncertainty of reception on the Vietnamese side which had waged skirmishes against the Khmer Rouge since 1976. In Vietnam they created a secret National Salvation Armed Forces which later became National United Salvation Front on 2 December 1978 and successfully overthrew Democratic Kampuchea regime on 7 January 1979.

Upon gaining control of Phnom Penh, the Front quickly formed on 8 January 1979 the Kampuchean People's Revolutionary Council (KPRC) as the transitional government, which later formed self-management committees in the villages. Led by Heng Samrin, the KPRC ruled Cambodia until June 27, 1981 when the newly established constitution replaced it with a Council of Ministers. On January 10, 1979, the Kampuchean People's Revolutionary Council (KPRC) announced that the official name of Cambodia was the People's Republic of Kampuchea (PRK). A week later the PRK notified the Security Council of the United Nations that it was the sole government of the Cambodian people.[1]

Vietnam was the first country to recognize the new regime. In February 1979, Vietnam and Cambodia signed a Treaty of Peace, Friendship and Cooperation, which declared that "peace and security of the two countries are closely interrelated and that the two Parties are duty-bound to help each other against all schemes and acts of sabotage by the imperialist and international reactionary forces."[2] The two governments also signed treaties for cooperation on economic, cultural, educational, public health and scientific and technological issues. The treaties would allow Vietnam to continue its occupation of Cambodia and provide support to it in all sectors. Vietnam would withdraw from

---

1   Margaret Slocomb, *The People's Republic of Kampuchea 1979-1989: The Revolution after Pol Pot,* Bangkok: Silkworm Books, 2004.
2   Russell R. Ross, ed. Cambodia: *A Country Study.* Washington: GPO for the Library of Congress, 1987.

Cambodia in 1990, sooner than projected in the Treaty.[3]

In January 1980, twenty nine such countries recognized the PRK; however, nearly eighty others did not, instead recognizing the (Coalition Government of Democratic Kampuchea) CGDK as the legitimate government of Cambodia. ASEAN countries – Indonesia, Malaysia, the Philippines and Singapore – led by Thailand, whose security was threatened by events in Cambodia and was now coping with humanitarian issues along the border, opposed the PRK.

The PRK had a huge task to complete in the 1980s including preventing the return of the Khmer Rouge and rebuilding Cambodia from the ashes of genocide. The economy had to be revived. Religious institution had to be reinstated. The PRK had to establish an elaborate network of orphanages to shelter hundreds of thousands of children whose parents were killed or were simply lost due to several rounds of evacuations by the Khmer Rouge.

Norng Chan Phal was one of the children being raised in such shelters. He was found by incoming soldiers in early January 1979 at S-21. He was emaciated and shaken but his spirit was high. Norng Chan Phal's story is a tale of resilience and a tremendous lesson for the younger generations to learn and to remember what happened under the Khmer Rouge regime. Such understanding of the darkness of genocide and appreciation of the sacrifices made to liberate Cambodian people from the abyss will provide impetus for promotion of peace and development.

---

3   Ibid.

1. THE EARLY YEARS

Norng Chan Phal (simply Phal or aka Lan) was born on 12 January 1970, in the year of the dog of the Khmer zodiac designation. In Cambodia, January is a cool and pleasant month with cool dry wind blowing from the north. This wind replaces the hot and wet air blowing from the southwest of Cambodia bringing much needed rain from the Indian Ocean. The rainy season lasted from May to October, while the dry season stretches from November to April with December and January being the coolest period of the year. Adapted to the climate, Khmer farmers usually farm only once a year during the rainy season and used the remaining parts of the year to conduct short-term cropping, trading and other activities.

Large Family

Phal was born in a coastal province of Cambodia in Damnak Snoul village, Sre Knong commune, Chum Kiri district, Kampot province, about 60 kilometer from Kampot town. He is not the only member of his family. Indeed, being the second youngest son, Phal had a large family. Along with him, his parents Norng Chen and Mom Yov gave birth to six other children including:

- Norng Sok Chea (aka Thnong), eldest sister, was born in 1952 and died with her baby and many other Cambodians in the turbulent period of early 1979 after stepping on a landmine while being evacuated by the Khmer Rouge to the Cambodian-Thai border.

- Norng Chen Than, eldest brother, was born on 1 October 1956, and is currently working in the Cambodian army and has five children.

- Norng Thaong (aka Kaot), older brother, was born on 2 May 1959

- Norng Kim Den, older brother, was born in 1964 (specific date unknown)

- Norng Kim Lorn (aka Train), older sister, was born on 15 June 1967 (specific date unknown)

- Norng Chan Phal (simply Phal or aka Lan), was born on 12 January 1970

- Norng Chan Ly (aka Lit), youngest son, was born on 2 February, 1973.

Norng Chan Phal's Family Diagram

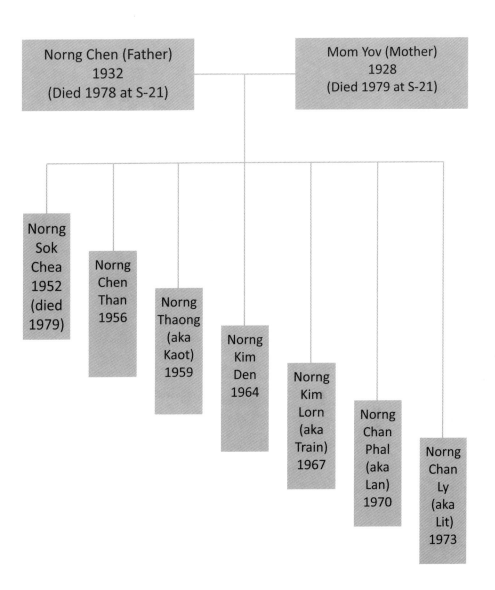

Norng Chen Than[4]

Norng Thaong (aka Kaot)[5]

5   *Photo courtesy of CIPD.*

Norng Kim Lorn (aka Train)[6]

---

7   *Photo courtesy of CIPD.*

Norng Chan Phal's father (Norng Chen) was four years younger than his mother. He was born in 1932 while his mother Mom Yov was born in 1928. Norng Chen was an experienced carpenter who was frequently involved in construction and other religious activities with the village pagodas. Phal's mother Mom Yov was a farmer and caring housewife. Having seven children, it was strenuous for her simply to keep track of them all but on the plus side she had helping hands on farming activities and animal care. During the 1960s and early 1970s, the family was apparently quite well off. Apart from carpentry business and farming, Phal's parents had up to 30 cows, 20 buffaloes and one elephant, an unusually acquisition for a rural family which generally had a few cattle for basic farming works. Having these many animals required a lot of attention but it was also not difficult as it is now as there were plenty of open field for the animals to forage for food. Nowadays many fields are owned by the locals or people from outside the village. Each of these animals had endearing names remembered clearly by Norng Chan Phal who always played with them like close friends after the animals returned home from a long day of works with his father at the construction sites and his mother at the farms.

The Bliss of Pre-War Years

Life as a boy in a typical Cambodian rural village was happy and it is especially so for Phal whose parents were doing well. Phal remembers that during a festive season his parents brought him and his siblings to Kampot town to attend a concert performance. It was a memorable sight and sound for him. As a young boy Norng Chan Phal liked to lick at the cool shaved ice topped with coconut milk and condensed milk or colorful syrup. Some vendors would use honey to add to the taste and top it with cashew or peanuts. Everyday vendor on the bicycle would arrive in front of his house at around 3 p.m. to sell the grounded ice to Chan Phal and his friends. Under the sheering heat of the day, the sweetened shaved ice provided much needed relief to the high temperature. Phal would do his best to ask for favors from his parents to get the shaved ice once it arrived.

Chan Phal's home province is a pleasant tourist destination among Cambodians and foreigners. Kampot province is 4.873 square kilometers with a sizable population of 620,000 between Buddhists majority and Muslim minority. The majority of the Muslims in Kampot originated from Malaysia and not from Champa like those living in Kampong Cham. These Muslims do not speak Cham language. The Buddhist population was a mix of Chinese descendants and Khmer origins. The Chinese having arrived between 1920s and 1940s by boat usually settled near the coast of Kampot town. Phal's family belongs to the Khmer Buddhist group.

Kampot Town

Kampot province is located in the Southwest of the country, having an eighty kilometers coastal strip and is bordering to the North with Kampong Speu, in the East with Takeo, in the West with Preah Sihanouk and Koh Kong provinces and to the South with the Gulf of Thailand. The East of the province consists of the typical plain area of Cambodia, covering rice fields and other agricultural plantations with fields of rice, corn, sesame and cassava while closer to the coast people grow the unique Kampot durian, rambutan, coconut and pepper taking advantage of the wet climate and fertile soil. The Western part of the province looms with the well-known majestic Bokor National Park, a Western part of the grand Elephant Mountains, which is rich in lush virgin forest and a huge range of rare wildlife. The highest point in the province is the Bokor Hill Station with 1,027m in altitude.

The provincial capital is named Kampot and sits near the base of the abundant green Elephant Mountains and the famous Bokor Hill Station. The Kampot area also has pre-Angkorian ruins and caves within adoring limestone mountains. These mountains provided Kampot another specialty in industrial production of cement which is different from the rest of Cambodia while closer to sea people make Kampot salt. Kampot town was originally built as a coastal colonial and vacation outpost has a French colonial architecture which is still in charming condition. The part of town along the Kampot river is lined with old buildings languishing in stately decay and adored by Western and Cambodian tourists. At one time, their strong, simple geometrical forms, high ceilings, hardwood floors, and mustard yellow walls symbolized both the simple orderliness and foreign grandeur of French administration.

The site of the renowned Bokor Hill Station was first accessed in 1916. In the years that followed, the French constructed a luxurious hill station there in order to escape the brutal heat and oppressive humidity of the tropics and enjoy the cool, fresh, and supposedly healthful air of higher altitudes. For many homesick colonials, the hilltops climate was a reminder of European summers. The community was inaugurated on February 14, 1925. Originally, there was a post office, a Catholic Church, a schoolhouse and residential buildings. French officials and Cambodian royalty took the convict-built road to the top. There they held opulent gatherings at the hotel and threw away fortunes at the celebrated casino. In its heyday, broken gamblers were rumored to have flung themselves from the casinos terrace and plummet to their deaths down the jungle-covered cliff overlooking the Gulf of Thailand.[8]

Wars closed Bokor colonial splendor several times. It was abandoned first in the 1940s, during the Vietnamese struggle for independence from the French, and then again in 1970 with the growing menace of the Khmer Rouge. Forces loyal to the Khmer Rouge took control of the mountain in 1972 and established an impregnable strategic military outpost well into the 1980s and 1990s. The road fell into disrepair, and mines were laid that rendered the site hazardous for decades.

---

8   Kitagawa Takako, "Kampot of the Belle Époque: From the Outlet of Cambodia to a Colonial Resort," *Southeast Asian Studies,* Vol. 42, No. 4, March 2005.

In 1979, the invading Vietnamese army engaged the Khmer Rouge on the site, and the vestiges of their outposts are still visible today. Following the end of Vietnamese occupation, the area around Kampot continued to suffer from remnants of wars. In 1994, Khmer Rouge soldiers attacked a passenger train bound for Sihanouk Ville. They slaughtered local passengers and abducted three foreigners, who were forced to endure slave labor while officials negotiated for their release and were finally taken into a secret location and shot.

Khmer Rouge's Administration of Kampot

Under the Khmer Rouge regime, Kampot was controlled by the infamous, supposedly long-lasting, determined, one-legged Khmer Rouge commander named Chhit Choeun (aka Ta Mok) who was the secretary of the southwest zone spanning Takeo, two districts of Kampong Speu (Kong Pisey and Samrong Tong), and five districts of Kandal province (Kandal Stung, Sa-ang, Koh Thom, Kean Svay, and Leuk Dek). It was then subdivided into four administrative regions designated by numbers 13, 33, 35 and 25.[9]

Ta Mok was born in 1926 in Takeo province. He spent several years during his adolescent period as a Buddhist monk. He married his cousin Uk Khoem and had had four children. In 1949, Ta Mok was head of a local anti-colonial Issarak movement and became a dedicated communist in 1963. Like many leaders among the Khmer Rouge's senior and most responsible officials for the death and suffering of the people, Ta Mok started off as a benign, people loving soldier. As the years progressed he became different and more ruthless. He lost one of his legs during a fighting in 1970, earning him reward and trust among Khmer Rouge leadership. From 1968 to 1978, Ta Mok was secretary of the expanding and shrinking Southwest zone. In November 1978,

---

9   David Chandler, Voices from S-21: Terror and History in Pol Pot's Secret Prison, Los Angeles: University of California Press, 1999.

Ta Mok was appointed as second deputy secretary of the CPK.[10]

After during the final years and after the collapse of the Khmer Rouge's political organization, Ta Mok never applied for amnesty and never attempted to defect. He was one of the remaining Khmer Rouge leaders who captured Pol Pot and put a weeping Brother Number One on trial in front of their own followers in 1997. As the Khmer Rouge apparatus collapsed, he was captured near the Thai border by the Cambodian army in March 1999 and was imprisoned. He died of disease on July 21, 2006 in captivity.[11]

As in other DK zones, there were the prisons, torture, executions, starvation and over-work. But by the end of the three years, eight months and 20 days of the regime, the Southwest had a particularly bloody reputation even by DK standards, in particular its role in conducting purges in other zones within Democratic Kampuchea. Ta Mok was known for his nicety to the people under his control, but extremely harsh against his perceived enemies or those designated as enemies by Angkar. Some people believed that Ta Mok never killed by himself. Although few people doubt Mok's role in the zone's killing machine, Tit Khem who served as a truck driver for the Khmer Rouge said: "I never saw Ta Mok kill anyone or order people to be killed. But I saw the commune authorities arrest people and take them to the detention centers. As a truck driver, I used to take people to the prisons in Takeo. I didn't know what was going to happen to them." Ta Mok was demanding on his people to deliver grand project results for him in the Southwest zone including a dam stretching about 14km in Kampot.

Between 1970 and 1975 a period in which the Khmer Rouge was expanding at the loss of Lon Nol's Khmer's Republic regime, Phal's family and others in the area were assigned into "mutual aid teams"

---

10 Peter Maguire, *Facing Death in Cambodia,* New York: Columbia University Press, 2005.
11 Stephen Heder and Brian Tittemore, *Seven Candidates for Prosecution: Accountability for the Crimes of the Khmer Rouge,* Phnom Penh: DC-Cam, 2001.

with members ranging from 50 to 150 persons consisting of 10 to 30 families. This grouping was again reorganized in 1973 into small co-operatives with several hundred members or covering an entire village or nearby villages. After the Khmer Rouge's victory in 1975, the co-operative system remained in place but then it reset and merged into even larger cooperatives in 1977 consisting of thousands of people within a commune.

The Cooperatives

The main purpose of the CPK's cooperatives was abolition of private ownership, capitalism and the old vestiges of the colonial and Lon Nol's practices. It was also to strengthen collectivity, farming activi-ties, the elevated status of workers and peasants, rural livelihood and selflessness. To the Khmer Rouge, a cooperative was meant to assign people to work, live and eat together as well as sharing properties, hard time and good time. Members of the cooperative had to give up all their property, which was their lifesaving and valuable means of income, to be used collectively. Such property included tools, cattle, plows, rakes, seed rice, and land. Phal's family suffered the unfair con-tribution of their animals and other belongings. The cooperatives were designed to be optimally self-sufficient. The Khmer Rouge leaders boosted that cooperatives were a great new forces of the revolution capable of building Cambodia as a modern agricultural utopia and protect Democratic Kampuchea against enemy infiltration.

Under the cooperative, life was supposed to be collective, fully ar-ranged, controlled and monitored by Angkar in all aspects. As with any drastic changes to social and familial organization, many people were affected in the worst way. Collectivity resulted in severe re-strictions on family and private life. Cambodian families had eaten together for thousands of years as parts of a family bonding process, so eating in cooperatives with little food created a sense of emptiness and displacement among many Cambodians. Resistance, mistakes and petty crimes were abundant and in turn creating a condition of constant suspicion among the Khmer Rouge officials themselves. Such condition was ripe for further repression, arrest, torture, reeducation and execution.

Base and New People

In other areas of their new social reorganization, the Khmer Rouge intended to create equality by eliminating their perceived old class system, yet they created a new class system nevertheless in the form "the base people" and "the new people."

The base people, or old people, were those who had lived in the countryside controlled by the Khmer Rouge for up to five years prior to their final control of Phnom Penh on April 17, 1975. The Khmer Rouge designated them as people with all the rights given by Angkar namely "full-rights". These people were further considered cleaner when they had no relatives working for the Khmer Republic regime of General Lon Nol and Prince Sirik Matak. They belong to the working class of the laborers and farmers and were usually economically poor prior to Khmer Rouge arrival. From 1975, these people were allowed to vote and to run for an election in March 20, 1976. Base people had more opportunities for promotion up the Khmer Rouge ranks and files. Those base people whose relatives live in Phnom Penh and work for Lon Nol were classed as "Candidates" who need to work harder within Democratic Kampuchea.

The new people, or 17 April people, were names given to the evacuees from the cities and towns during the Khmer Rouge's grandiose displacement of national population in three days. This group mostly consisted of urban dwellers from Phnom Penh and other town centers but also included people from the countryside and had moved to the cities to escape the war, bombings, famine or simply impending Khmer Rouge's harsh control. New people were considered suspicious and viewed by Angkar as potential sources of protest and rebellions against the Khmer Rouge rule. In this way, they were sometimes called "parasites" and had little rights as a Khmer Rouge slogan asserted: "17 April people are parasitic plants. They are the losers of the war and prisoners of war." New people received harshest treatment from the Khmer Rouge and also depending on where they were sent to and who controlled them. People in the East zone were treated better than those evacuated to the Northwest zone.[12]

---

12 Henri Locard, *Pol Pot's Little Red Book: The Sayings of Angkar,* Bangkok: Silkworm Books, 2004.

2. JOURNEY INTO THE EYE OF THE TYPHOON

The words "Khmer Rouge" was the fateful name given to communist groups in Cambodia by Prince Norodom Sihanouk in the 1960s.[13] His clearest mention of this term occurred in 1967 in relation to the presence and increasing influence of the communists in rural areas of Cambodia. In Prince Sihanouk's Khmerization campaign, which attempted to conflate Cambodia's myriad identity groups into one large Khmer identity, both the communists, ethnic highlanders, Chinese, Vietnamese and other ethnic groups were given a Khmer label, just like many other social and political groups in Cambodia.

For the prince, there was undeniable equality among all peoples in Cambodia, but the Khmer Rouge saw it differently. They saw economic injustice and exploitation of the poor by the rich, of the illiterate by the educated, and of rural farmers by urban dwellers. Royalism, feudalism, capitalism and modernity were to be eliminated. A new Khmer identity was needed to liberate Cambodia from its social ills and launch it into the Khmer Rouge's own "modern and progressive" future in which everyone was equal, and there were no crimes, no social classes, no rich, no poor and no diversity.

Sihanouk tried to conflate Cambodia's identity groups into one huge Khmer group, but he respected their subordinate identities, for example, by appending to the term Khmer a marker that differentiated whether one was a Chinese, hill tribesman, communist or liberal. However, for the Khmer Rouge, there was no such sub-identity.

Before 1970 the Khmer Rouge was considered to be a politically and militarily weak communist group. They relied heavily on logistical and political support from North Vietnam.[14] Khmer communists and communists elsewhere in Indochina inevitably had relationships. When

13 Khamboly Dy, *A History of Democratic Kampuchea 1975-1979*, Phnom Penh: Documentation Center of Cambodia, 2007.
14 David Chandler, *A History of Cambodia*, Bangkok: Silkworm Books, 1993.

the first Indochina war broke out, a group was formed in 1950 called the Khmer Issarrak, which was led by Khmer communists. They were closely aligned with Ho Chi Minh's communist guerillas. Even the Khmer People's Revolutionary Party received advice from Vietnam when it was being created a year later.[15]

The future supreme leader of Democratic Kampuchea, Pol Pot, was still in France at this time and played no part in these early political movements. He would return to Cambodia from studying in France in 1953. The early communists in Cambodia were led by Son Ngoc Minh, Siv Heng, Tou Samuth and Chan Samay. Upon independence from France in 1953 and the end of First Indochinese War in 1954, communism became less tolerated by Prince Norodom Sihanouk. As a result, some of the communist leaders fled to Vietnam.[16]

The communists also created a political party called the People's Party to compete in a 1955 national election with Sihanouk's Sangkum Reastr Niyum Party. Pol Pot was then active in this process and he tasted his first political defeat.[17] His party and the Democrat Party which he supported failed by a landslide. Prince Sihanouk emerged as an undisputed victor in the election. This gave Pol Pot a valuable lesson about the power and popularity of the Prince. He also learned about party loyalty and how to enforce it when members of his communist movements began to defect to Prince Sihanouk's new regime. Siv Heng, a leader of the Khmer People's Revolutionary Party, defected in 1959.[18] His defection was followed by the arrests of many secret communists. But by then the communists had established a strong base in Kampong Cham and Takeo provinces. These two provinces would later be expanded to become the Eastern and Southwest Zones, the two Khmer Rouge zones where there would be disastrous consequences for the Cham.

---

15 Ibid.
16 Khamboly Dy, *A History of Democratic Kampuchea 1975-1979*, op. cit.
17 David Chandler, *Brother Number One: A Political Biography of Pol Pot*, Boulder: Westview Press, 1999.
18 Khamboly Dy, *A History of Democratic Kampuchea 1975-1979*, op. cit.

In 1962 Pol Pot became the full-fledged leader of the communists in Cambodia with Nuon Chea as his deputy. Pol Pot immediately fled to the least inhabited northeast area of Cambodia. He would later call it the Northeast Zone. There he recruited hill tribesmen to fight for communism. He visited Vietnam, China and North Korea in 1965.[19] The visit was a revelation for him. It showed him the difference between various brands of communism. By then China and the Soviet Union had begun to show signs of serious disagreement. Pol Pot returned to northeast Cambodia after becoming disenchanted and disgusted with the prospect of a unified Communist Party of Indochina. In 1966, he formed the Communist Party of Kampuchea. As evidence of his distrust for Vietnam, Cambodian communists trained in Vietnam would gradually be alienated, imprisoned and secretly executed.

The elimination of long-term communist members inevitably weakened communist movements. It also brought in the discrepancies of interpreting and implementing communism in Cambodia. In addition, it led to variations in practice in different parts of the country. Such variations further weakened the communist movement. But Pol Pot's luck changed in March 1970 when Lon Nol and Sisowath Sirik Matak (Sihanouk's uncle) deposed the prince in a bloodless coup while Sihanouk was on a trip to France.[20] Not only was Sihanouk humiliated by his own subordinates, but if he returned to Cambodia he would face prosecution and imprisonment. He had no choice but to side with Pol Pot's communist movement, which by then had fairly well established armed guerrilla pockets around the country. Siding with the communists, Sihanouk also allowed Pol Pot's communist movement to take advantage of his overwhelming rural popularity. This radically changed the communist's manpower as well as its military capability.[21]

---

19 David Chandler, Brother Number One: *A Political Biography of Pol Pot,* op. cit.

20 Henry Locard disagrees that this was a coup, as parliament voted Prince Sihanouk from power in the same year.

21 Ben Kiernan, *The Pol Pot Regime: Race, Power and Genocide in Cambodia under the Khmer Rouge, 1975-1979,* op. cit.

But Pol Pot made sure he was the one who had the power, not Sihanouk. The coup in 1970 also plunged Cambodia into the Second Indochina War and split it into what the Khmer Rouge termed the liberated zone and the Lon Nol zone.

Like many Cambodians, Norng Chan Phal's family was caught between these zones. By 1972 almost 70% of Cambodia's territory was controlled by the Khmer Rouge. Lon Nol controlled the seaports, the coast, roads linking Phnom Penh and South Vietnam, and parts of Kampong Chhnang, Pursat and Battambang provinces linking Phnom Penh with Thailand.[22] By 1973 almost 90% of Cambodia was controlled by the Khmer Rouge.[23] Lon Nol forces controlled only the roads linking Phnom Penh with Sihanouk seaport, with Kampong Cham and Battambang. The only large visible territory controlled by Lon Nol at this time was along the Thai border in Battambang province. Several provincial towns were also still under his army's control, including Kampong Cham, Kampot, Kampong Thom, Pursat, Siem Reap, Sihanouk Ville, Prey Veng, Svay Rieng, Kandal and Battambang, although these towns were isolated.[24] However, these territories were heavily infiltrated by covert communists. Even Lon Nol officers were known to have conducted business with the communists.

---

22 DC-Cam Document: Khmer Rouge Liberated Zone May 1972.
23 DC-Cam Document: Khmer Rouge Liberated Zone May 1973.
24 Ibid.

Area Controlled by the Khmer Rouge in 1972[25]

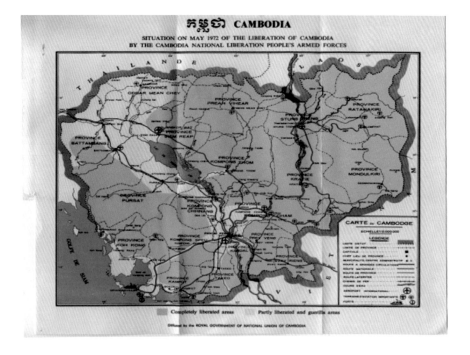

The War Was Over

The Khmer Rouge finally gained control of the entire country on April 17, 1975 when Phnom Penh fell in a bloodless final stage of the war. A number of radical plans were then implemented by the Khmer Rouge to keep Cambodians from rebelling and to achieve their grandiose long-term vision of a utopian Cambodia. Phnom Penh and other town centers were evacuated. Nuon Chea later mentioned during his testimony before the ECCC (Extraordinary Chambers in the Courts of Cambodia, popularly known as the Khmer Rouge Tribunal) that this was done to control the people. Men, women, and children, and even hospital patients and the elderly, were ordered to leave by foot to the countryside. However, the Khmer Rouge did not have a specific plan

---

25 DC-Cam Archives.

of how to divide people. They just knew that towns had to be dispersed to the countryside. In Phnom Penh, people chose to walk along major highways to the villages where they used to live or had close relatives. However, because a curfew was imposed, some people could not travel to the village of their choice. Furthermore, they expected to return to Phnom Penh within a few days.

In December 1975, Khmer Rouge leaders and officials met to discuss the creation of a new national Constitution which they passed in January 1976.[26] In the same year Democratic Kampuchea eliminated the old administrative divisions and created new divisions based on zones, regions, districts, communes and villages. They created 6 zones with 32 regions. In 1976, Democratic Kampuchea officials also met to create a four-year plan to be implemented from 1977 to 1980 in which agriculture was the main production priority, to be achieved via collectivization, cooperative units and de-privatization.[27] However, the implementation of similar forms of cooperatives in some villages began much earlier. Depending on their ages, members of families were separated into children's, mobiles, women's, men's and elderly units, among others.

Norng Chan Phal's home village in Kampot province had been controlled by the Khmer Rouge guerillas since 1970. His village was classed into a notorious Khmer Rouge southwest zone controlled by Ta Mok. During the evacuation of Phnom Penh in April 1975, his family was expelled from home and moved to a village called Treng Trayeng, Phnom Srouch district, Kampong Speu province. Kampong Speu province is located about 45 kilometer west of Phnom Penh. It borders Kampong Chhnang and Pursat to the North, Phnon Penh to the East, Kampot and Takeo to the South and Koh Kong to the West. Speu is the Khmer word for star fruit, but Kampong Speu is actually famous for its palm sugar and wine. Kampong Speu is also home to the Kirirom

---

26 DC-Cam Document D21642: National Constitution of Democratic Kampuchea.
27 DC-Cam Document D00480: Study the Four-Year Plan.

National Park locating on a seven hundred meters hill covering an area of over thirty five thousand hectares in the Elephant Mountains.

The name "Kirirom" meaning Mountain of Joy was given to it by Late-King Father Norodom Sihanouk who constructed winding roads to the top of the mountain. This place is known for its unique high altitude pine trees which grow from a certain elevation on the mountain. The park also forms the headwaters for numerous streams feeding Kampong Speu districts, thus making the streams in the province highly unpredictable due to rainfall on the mountains and abrupt flows cascading down the hills. Norng Chan Phal found that out the hard way when he tried to escape the child unit which he was placed to visit his mother in another village during the night.

Under the Khmer Rouge regime, Kampong Speu province (except Kong Pisey and Samraong Tong districts) was placed under the Western Zone (Zone 401) with Chuo Chet serving as its secretary. This zone also encompassed Koh Kong and Kampong Chhnang provinces. The Western Zone covered five regions which were designated by numbers 31, 32, 37, 15, and 11.

The Western Zone was created later. It had been part of the Southwest Zone which had initially included Takeo, Kampot, Kompong Chhnang, Koh Kong, and Kompong Speu provinces. The Southwest zone was controlled by the infamous one-legged Khmer Rouge commander by the name of Ta Mok. Chou Chet was Ta Mok's deputy-secretary of the zone before the creation of the Western zone. He was also considered Ta Mok's competitor. Chou Chet had joined the revolutionary since 1954 and later imprisoned for his communist activities by Prince Norodom Sihanouk. By mid-1975, Southwest zone was separated into two parts controlled separately by Ta Mok and Chou Chet. Ta Mok controlled most of the Zone where there were many people and agricultural activities including Takeo and Kampot.

Chou Chet controlled Koh Kong, Kompong Speu, and Kompong Chnang, What he inherited was one of the poorest regions in Cambodia with infertile soil and little rain as it lied behind the mountains blocking rain water blowing from the gulf of Thailand but with more flood hazard than other places. The area he controlled eventually became the Western zone with a man named Ben Soeun acting as his the security commander and a member of the zone's central committee. Chou Chet's wife by the name of Ly held an important position within the zone. Chou Chet lived modest life in a small thatch-roofed cottage surrounded by coconut trees a few kilometers north of national road 4 in Kampong Speu province.

According to a witness named Nou Mao, who is now 82 and joined the revolution in the regime's Southwest Zone in 1971, said that Chou Chet vehemently opposed the evacuation of people from cities to the villages and between provinces to disconnect communication and confuse people. Such implementation would weaken the populace. In a study session which Nou Mao attended he witnessed the argument between Ta Mok and Chou Chet. He said: "Ta Mok talked about the evacuation of people in Phnom Penh. Chou Chet said people should not be evacuated. Some people didn't agree with the evacuation—they said that city dwellers wouldn't know about farming, and that they'd be allowed to stay wherever they wanted. People with opposing ideas to the evacuation would be reprimanded by Ta Mok on several occasions. He said the plan involved the whole country, not zones. Everyone had to be evacuated from cities." He added that "Khieu Samphan was also in favor of evacuation, while his cohorts, Hu Nim and Hu Youn, were not. So when these people [Hun Nim and Hu Youn] came to Phnom Penh, they died at Tuol Sleng prison."[28]

---

28 Mr Nou Mao, aka Mouk, 78, appeared as a witness in case 002/1 on June 19-20 2013 at the ECCC. He worked in military and then as a commune official. He testified about the study sessions by senior KR leaders such as Chou Chet and Ta Mok, the treatment of Khmer Viet Minh, and the opinions of senior KR leaders regarding the evacuation of Phnom Penh six months prior to its occurrence.

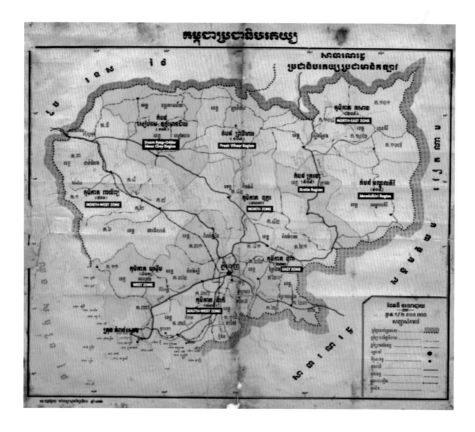

However, the Khmer Rouge's arrival and final capitulation of the Lon Nol regime was warmly welcome by the people especially when the Khmer Rouge announced publicly that their communist regime was clean, absolute, had no repression, had no exploitation, no class system, no rich and poor, no ranking. Everybody was equal before the Angkar (Khmer Rouge government). The regime gave highest values to the working class namely the workers and farmers. They ordered people to live in cooperatives, working together to achieve common targets, eating together as one family and loving each other as blood

29 DC-Cam archives.

siblings. They also required absolute loyalty from the people. All valuables were collected and placed as common properties of the cooperatives. Norng Chan Phal's parents had to give up their most valuable assets which were the cattles and elephant. These animals were later used in a logging factory which Khmer Rouge assigned his father as a supervisor. His mother was assigned to work as a cook in the factory kitchen.

Children Were Separated from Parents

Every night from 7 to 9 pm, the Khmer Rouge always called upon people in the cooperative to attend livelihood meeting to indoctrinate them about the essence of the revolution, to love the communist utopia, to make sacrifices, to abandon material needs, to be loyal toward Angkar, to dare to report to unit chief and to criticize and self-criticize people in the same unit. Procrastination and laziness in work must be avoided. In particular Angkar asked people to hate the intellectuals and those who repressed others and profited from other people's sweat and blood without using their own labor. Teachers, professors, monks, doctors, traders, feudalists, imperialists were included.

The Khmer Rouge considered them as the hardliners of the old regime who were difficult to change. People with fair skin whose parents were Chinese and Vietnamese and skilful in business were to be put outside of Angkar's range of acceptance. The Khmer Rouge hated the idea of buying low and selling high in the business transactions conducted mostly by the Chinese and Vietnamese ethnic groups. Thus the Khmer Rouge made a decision to sweep and clean these people, divide them into smaller groups, dispersed them to different places and finally placed their family members into different working units. They were closely watched by the Khmer Rouge militia and were usually the first to be blamed for all the wrongs within the cooperatives. When they made mistakes which one would consider simple such as breaking farming tools, stealing potatoes or rice, harvesting their own garden vegetables, and were caught red handed they could be executed.

As for children, they must have a resolute mind, abandon sentimentalism and sympathy for the enemies. Children were considered by the Khmer Rouge as pure and refined. They were the blank slate of papers waiting to be written by Angkar's ideological theories and accept Angkar as the new parents. The Khmer Rouge were successfully to some degrees in transforming innocent and impressionable children into killing machines, obedient executions or simply workers in the Khmer Rouge production process which revolved around rice production all year round.

As the Khmer Rouge began tightening the populace and exerting controls in social, economic, cultural and even personal life of the people, Norng Chan Phal was just six years old. Life was happy, simple and full of intrigues. It was supposed to be the beginning of his school year which he would have received basic education just like normal kids would have received. Under the Khmer Rouge's control, his childhood and all its dreams were swept into one universal matrix manipulated by the Angkar. Phal was swiftly put into a child unit along with other children who were about the same age. Some were older and a few were younger. They all had wide eyes waiting to be told, taught and led, perhaps with some work and play. Their impressionable minds were easy to be indoctrinated with little degree of resisting moral judgment. Phal's child unit was led by an older person usually in the early 20th. Everything the child unit chief told them and taught them every day over a period of several months were absorbed with little resistance like a sponge. The duty of the child unit including collecting manure for the farm, cutting shrub and making organic fertilizer, some basic literacy education under a large tree or any available huts within the village, along with basic revolutionary principles, especially to discriminate against those people with fair complexion arriving from Phnom Penh or other town centers.

As a smart village boy, Phal learnt fast in the arts of survival which he had to in order to survive under the cruel Khmer Rouge regime. The ways the Khmer Rouge put in place harsh lessons and controls on all members of Cambodians created new ways of lives and living conditions which killed so many people mostly formerly urban people or new people who had never experience harsh lives under the sun with very little food to eat and no modern medical care. Even some unprepared "base people" were caught by surprise by the new way of life placed by the Khmer Rouge and found it hard to live by. Phal's new village in Kampong Speu province was remote and locating in the southwest part of the province. The distance between his home village in Kampot province and the new village in Kampong Speu province was about 50 kilometer. His family had to walk to arrive at a new place in Kampong Speu. Surrounding environment did not really change and so it was easy for Phal to learn to identify plants and fruits that could be eaten as supplements to the poor and inadequate food ration provided in the Khmer Rouge's cooperative dining hall.

The Khmer Rouge regime concentrated much of the manpower of the entire country to grow rice and a few other plants. During the period of three years and eight months under their control, they organized people and tools into farming cycles including digging irrigation canal, building dams, pumping waters, plowing rice field, spreading seed, transplanting rice seedlings, fertilizing the field and harvesting the rice. With such concentrated effort, one would have believed that people would at least have sufficient rice to eat all year round. But it was not the case. There was barely enough food for everyone. Starvation was the main theme. The struggle to find food secretly by the people was perpetual. Young and old cooperative members had to find all possible ways to catch insects, lizards and other small animals to eat whenever possible at the risk of death. They had to dig for roots and tubers and pick tree leaves to eat on the go.

For both adult and children, food was provided in very small portion. Children in the child units had to forage for food during shrub collection trips or time off from basic education in or near the village. Phal slowly learnt that in the bush around his village, there were many plants and animals that were edible and could be caught. Phal learnt to identify many fruits that could be used in some ways as foods including Chumpou, Kuy, Punleak, Korkoh, Krolanh, Kantout, and Chey. Ngieng fruit and Kor leaves were used as shampoo. Plants with tubers including Thlong, Chorchak, Andaek and potato varieties could be collected in the bush. These plants were usually hidden among other trees. He could see theirs leaves on larger trees and began searching for the contacts with the ground. The smell, tastes and feel of these fruits, tubers and leaves remained a vivid and pleasant memory in Phal's brain as knowing them and obtaining them gave him a survival edge during the Khmer Rouge famine.

Secret Nocturnal Visit to His Mother

Living in a child unit for so many months gave Phal a dire yearning to meet his beloved mother. For Phal his father was a dedicated family man who dedicated much of his life to make sure his family was well fed and happy. With such dedication, Phal spent most of his days under the close care of his mother. Naturally he was closer to his mother than his father. During time of hardship, Phal wanted to see first and foremost Mom Yov who was assigned into a unit located several kilometers away from where he was. With such desire, everyday Phal always thought about ways to meet her and perhaps his father and siblings but the unit chief never allowed him that opportunity even if he asked many times. The main reasons behind the chief's denial was that Angkar had replaced Phal's parents as the guardians for him and that nobody else was above Angkar or more caring for Phal. Phal did not buy the reasoning. For him, it was too soon to forget her and to accept the idea of Angkar who he never met.

One day children were asked to work very hard in collecting plants at places further away from the village. They were brought back to the cooperative after sunset. As normal, the children were not allowed to eat the puny rice gruel or other wild vegetable soup right away. They were briefed repeatedly with revolutionary ideals and principles. There was also discussion about disciplines within the child unit. The meeting continued until 9 pm, followed by a late dinner. The children immediately went to bed and slept soundly as soon as their heads touched the mats. Phal was the exception. He did not sleep; he waited for the right opportunity to run away to see his mother in another village. He lied down but kept himself away until all the children including unit chief were deep in their sleep. When midnight came, he slowly got up and trudged through the maze of sleeping young fellows. He slowly opened the door and walked into the dark with only stars providing the faintest light. As a child, Phal was not afraid of superstitious beings or wild creatures, at least that was what he thought when he began the escape.

Phal walked a few kilometers on village walk paths winding down to meet national road 4. From that point he walked West to East toward his mother village. Phal had learnt about the direction several months ago when his mother came to see him. Without any note, he memorized the ways his mother told him. During the day, he had also learnt the environment surrounding his village, the connecting routes and dividing streams. Somehow, only a short moment after his nocturnal mini adventure, the unit chief followed him on a bicycle and took him back to the shelter. The next day, the unit chief told him to be resolute and severe any connections he had with his parents and siblings. Phal had to transform himself to be one of Angkar's sons completely.

A few months later, Phal had forgotten all that the chief told him about the parent Angkar. His yearning to meet his mother had rebounded. Alone in the cottage, Phal cried several times calling for mother and what she normally had given him to console his pain. It reached a point where he would risk harsh punishment to meet her and that Phal would escape again whenever there was a good chance to escape. Phal had learnt his mistakes in his previous escape. He chose well used paths and that when his escape became it would take only a few minutes for his unit chiefs on bicycle to find him on the road. During the day Phal learnt about the bushes between villages and he would try walking through it rather than the walk paths. Walking through the bushes would make it difficult for the chief to catch up and locate him.

During a rainy night with thundering sound of monsoon rain with occasional thunders, he saw his opportunity. Monsoon would pour a large amount of water in large falling droplets in a short period time. It would flood any stream close to the hill quickly. But it was also an opportunity for many people to collect water for use in dry spells. Rain water also has a distinct sweat taste enjoyed by many. Without acidity of today, rain water was much more pleasant than chlorinated tab water. Phal's unit chief lighted the torch and woke up the older children to collect falling water from the roof and fill in several large jars.

The loud noise and the wet created a perfect unsuspicious condition for an escape. As the rain became harder, the lightning became louder and the torch was doused, he crept out through an open back door in the dark. Phal could only see the road through the momentary flashes of lightning but he had remembered his surrounding well. Phal trotted the bush was clear and talked when it got a bit thicker. A moment later, Phal arrived a creek. In his escape plan, this dry creek was supposed to be crossed by a short dash down the bank and emerged the other bank. It had been completely dry a few days ago. Tonight it was overflowed with raging water. The heavy rain and lightning had handed him the opportunity but it now created a hazard that could kill him and foil his escape plan again. Still young, Phal had never swam in strong water before. He used to dip in shallow pond water and occasionally waded to the deep and swam back. This raging creek water was horrendous. Crossing it would be suicide. But the yearning to meet his mother was too great and going back to meet the unit chief again was completely foolish for Phal.

Phal came up with a strategy. Flowing water would sweep him down stream but if he could keep his head above the water long enough along with some paddling he would reach the other side of the bank downstream, provided the water flew in a calm way. Phal jumped took several steps back, walked up the bank and jumped into the water as far into the creek as possible. Then he began to float and push the water with his hands. As he fell into the water, the flood dragged him nearly 30 meters down the length of the creek. As he struggled and breathed through his mouth, he swallowed water. He tried to hold onto a branch or tree roots on the other to pull him toward the bank in the final effort. Phal said, "I thought I was going to die until I grabbed onto a thorny bamboo twig on the other side of the bank. It was my lifeline and I tried my best to not let go as my legs were dragged off the bottom." As his other hand found another bamboo branch he was able to pull his body up the bank slowly until he was above the water. Phal inspected his body which was poked with numerous bamboo thorns. It was bleeding and painful. The adrenaline, the fear of being caught, the longing for mother and the falling rain blocked his fear and the pain. Instead he was jubilating to have won the overflowing river and was ready to continue his journey to see his beloved mother.

As he walked forward the rain began to subside from deafening fall to drizzle. A moment later it stopped completely. In Cambodia, the monsoon rain normally falls strong and hard. Once it completes pouring down all the water, it would stop completely as if there isn't any happened before. It was case for the rain that night. As the rain stop and the sky began to open up, Phal could see some stars which helped lighting his way forward. As a young boy, Phal was brave but at the back of his head he had fear of the supernatural, wild beasts and other unexpected beings. Phal walked faster in order to get to the edge of his mother's village. A moment later, he heard the sound of the wolves in the distance. Kampong Speu was mostly plain which allowed habitation by the people. Immediately beyond the villages, high untamed mountains appeared from the jungle. Kampong Speu has the highest mountain in Cambodia, which is mount Oral at 1813 meter. The wolves kept howling which terrified me. As a young boy, the wolves were the scariest thing in the forest for Phal. As he got closer to the village, the sound began to fade.

About an hour later, Phal finally reached his mother's cottage. She had brought him once before after asking permissions from her women mobile unit chief to take Phal for treatment. Phal had been weak and sick. Phal had stayed for a few days so he remembers exactly where it was among the other palm leave cottages in the village. As Phal arrived his mother's house, he did not knock or make any sound. He walked around it and found a hole in the leave wall. He crawled through it and entered the cottage. He found his mother sleeping inside. Phal loved his mother although she had rules and disciplines. He did not wake her up. He instead lied down and slept below her feet with his wet clothes. It was a warming moment to be by his mother at last. He felt comfortable and safe. Touching his mother's feet, he had everything he needed at that moment.

Mom Yov feeling the cold of Phal's wet clothes began to move around and woke up to inspect it. She thought it was a wet cat seeking warmth beside her or something creepy crawlies from the forest. Normally after a huge rain, snakes, insects and other animals would move to higher ground to escape flood. They would find a warm and dry cottage ideal of hiding. Mom Yov got up, lighted a candle and point it toward the end of her mat. There it was a young boy sleeping with wet clothes pulling his hands and feet together in a bundle. She was shocked to see her shivering son sleeping next to her. She said, "Oh my beloved son! It is so far from your place and you made it here in the middle of a rainy night. How could you take this dangerous journey?" Phal told her everything. Mom Yov took out dry towel, took off Phal's clothes and covered him. In mother's care, Phal needed not think about anything else. He did not need to be independent and worry any more.

Unbeknown to Phal, immediately after he left my cottage, the unit chief noticed that Phal was missing. He began looking for him with the help of older children in the unit. As they searched, they found footprints of Phal and including those tigers and wolves near the creek. They assumed that Phal would have been eaten by the wild beasts. Fearing for their safety, they stopped searching and returned to the sleeping quarter. The next morning, his mother told her cooperative colleagues about his rendezvous to meet her in the middle of the night through dangerous bushes. They were all surprised at the success and bravery of the trip. Later in the day, my mother returned Phal to the child unit. The unit chief was also shocked to see Phal. He did not punished Phal for the secret trip but was happy to see him alive back in the unit. Phal's unit chief was one of those kind hearted persons within the Khmer Rouge regime. Within the genocidal Democratic Kampuchea, there were good and vengeful Khmer Rouge members. Khmer Rouge officials fought between being placing radicalized policies on the people and moderate social changes to ease adaptation. Normally the good ones were arrested and executed by the more radical and fierce leaders. Those Khmer Rouge members who were arrested were brought to the infamous S-21 prison in Phnom Penh. It was a place reserved for victims of Khmer Rouge's purges of their fellow but allegedly traitorous revolutionaries.

Love for Household Animals

Phal always had a loving relationship with his family's animals. As a carpenter and farmer, his parents thought it was wise to keep large animals to lighten the load of the family even when we had up to 30 cows, 20 buffaloes and one elephant. Back then in my home village in Kampot province, there was plenty of open field and bushes for the animal to wander during the day to find leaves and grass to eat. It was easy to keep cattle and buffalos. His parents with the help of his elder brothers simply release them in the morning and collect them back in late afternoon. His elders brothers did much of the cattle tending. As a young boy, Phal simply tagged along his brothers as they left home with the cattle and played along the way. Of particular fondness for Phal was the lone female elephant. The animal was huge. Phal's parents bought it from a family of elephant breeders in another part of the province. That breeders perhaps caught a few elephants from the mountains and tamed them. Phal's parents named the elephant Sok. Phal always fed her banana or watermelon skin by hand which she would reach out with her long, sensitive trunk to grab it and chew the food as if it was the most delicious thing on earth. Phal liked to touch the elephant and feel her sick hide with a few large fur here and there. Phal's parents would use the elephant occasionally to pull large log and to transport wood to construction site

As the Khmer Rouge arrived in Phal's home village, they began instructing them to place all the animals collectively for all to use. They even slaughtered some of the cows for food and blamed Phal's parents for being individualistic and greedy for having so many animals without allocating them for other villagers. The Khmer Rouge did not implement what they said at first as it was early to fracture their loving relationship with the people before complete victory was assured. As Phnom Penh felt, Phal and his family were told to move to Kampong Speu with all the animals. It was extremely difficult for his brothers and parents to herd large animals by foot. It took several tiring days to get to the final destination which the Khmer Rouge selected in a village in Kampong Speu.

Immediately upon arrival, the animals were placed under the control of the cooperatives. A few more cows were slaughtered to provide food for the cadres, soldiers and village chiefs. A small portion was allocated to the cooperative kitchen for the people. As owners Phal's family took only a small part without complaint. The world had changed. What viewed as ownership of private individuals became properties of the mass. It was not really the mass though as the Khmer Rouge's cooperative committee took much of the share. The remaining animals were put to work at a sawmill which Norng Chen was assigned to lead the work there. With years of experience in woodwork, Norng Chen was perfectly suited to the job. At least he could continue to control the use of his valuable animals especially the elephants which required specialist care for its wellbeing.

Whenever Phal walked past the sawmill, he always tried to look for the elephant and called her name. Upon hearing its name, the elephant looked at him and tried to walk. But she was not allowed much sentiment with Phal. It was a time of resoluteness and little personal connection, be it with persons or animals. Angkar was the only object of love, loyalty and respect. Angkar decided what to love, who to marry, what to do, what to eat and what to learn. It was a time of tight and meticulous control of life in all aspects. What Phal had for a simple relationship with his elephant was calling name and brief look at each other. Phal soon walked pass the sawmill and the elephant kept looking for him until he walked out of sight. Even his father could not talk much to his son during work. He was quiet and focused on his assignment.

Phal noticed that with his father's best care, his animals were in poorer condition everyday due to overwork and poor nutrition despite the fact that there was plenty of bushes and field for them to forage. Suggestion for the wellbeing of the animals was not heeded. The Khmer Rouge had drastically altered the Khmer society and yet they placed most illiterate people in leadership positions from national and sub-national levels. With so much parameters to observe and orders to stick to, the cooperative committee failed in many aspects of the new society. People felt ill without medicine which the Khmer Rouge did their best to eliminate and replaced it with what they called "rabbit droppings" medicine. Animals became emaciated. Rice harvest was poor without modern fertilization and large machinery to help in large production process. Other crops such as cassava and vegetables did not yield well. Adding to lack of knowledge, the Khmer Rouge was particularly paranoia about suggestions that could jeopardize their revolution. Everyone in the cooperative from boys to men, women and the elderlies were considered as potential spies and enemies infiltrators. Phal informed his mother about their animals. She could do nothing beside taking a deep breath and sympathizing them. His father did what he could. But his preoccupation at the time was survival of his family members. The animals although was valuable before the Khmer Rouge became his least important priority. He hoped to keep working and obeying Angkar's orders until the time come for this radical regime to be toppled in some ways.

Mom Yov Fell Ill

The Khmer Rouge's radical policy of forcing everybody to be a member of a gigantic agricultural production process especially using available local means was devastating for the country's population. The Khmer Rouge's grand theory of self-reliance was the main principle behind this. They said to be independent in all sectors, Cambodia has to be able to make their own food and not import from a foreign country. This principle also trickled down to other aspects of development and health care.

Being forced to work hard continuously for several months with little food to eat, Phal's mother fell ill. Her limbs became swollen due to malnutrition and salt. Salt was a rare commodity under the Khmer Rouge regime. Some people would dig up root of coconut tree and boil it to get to the evaporated salt. Considering Cambodia has 450 km of coastline, lacking salt tells so much story about the Khmer Rouge's ability to distribute resources to the right places for those who needed them. Phal's home province of Kampot along the coast had been the center of salt production. From there salt was transported to all parts of Cambodia. Kampong Speu was not that far away from the sea, but still people did not have enough salt to eat. With each passing day, Mom

Yov's condition deteriorated and she could not walk, let alone work. In this situation she was facing the threat of being executed for being weak, lazy or simply left out by the revolution. The sick was considered both feeble and irresolute toward the ideals of the revolution.[30]

Compounding the problem of lack of food and illnesses resulting from malnutrition, the Khmer Rouge did not have a working hospital especial at the cooperative level. There were a few rudimentary hospitals at the zonal and regional levels. Even there the healthcare facility was poor with very few trained doctors and nurses. Upon victory on April 17, 1975, the Khmer Rouge purged doctors, abandoned existing modern healthcare facility and adopted traditional medicine instead. It was what they called "rabbit droppings" medicine (thnam ach tunsay). Khmer traditional medicine was still at a basic level and required scientific research for its use to be effective, consistent and targeted. Traditional Khmer doctors only know illnesses and a broad array of plants including roots, barks, leaves, flowers and fruits which could be prescribed for such illnesses. The Khmer Rouge utilized this traditional knowledge and implemented it all over Cambodia.[31]

The backbone of the Khmer Rouge's traditional medical team was revolutionary women from the base area including Takeo province in the Southwest Zone. Women in Tram Kak district, Takeo province, were ordered to supervise other women from various regions in medical skills. Many nurses and staff in Phnom Penh's hospitals and medical factories came from Tram Kak district and other districts in Takeo province. These women were given additional privileges and responsibilities because they had received political education from the party before many others during the war period.

Medicine was a skill that women in the Democratic Kampuchea want-

---

30 Author's interview with Chea Phal in Anlong Veng district, 30 June 2012.
31 Kok-Thay ENG, "Anlong Veng Then and Now: A Story of Its People," *Searching for the Truth, 9 July 2012,* Phnom Penh: DC-Cam.

ed to learn, since it gave them class prestige. Although the Khmer Rouge neglected healthcare, the health profession was glorified by the Khmer Rouge and was second in status after defense. A Khmer Rouge slogan said, "Daughters should grow up to be medical staff, while sons, to be soldiers." Most importantly Angkar asserted that "a revolutionary medical staff has to originate from peasant families." According to interviews with former medical staff in Tram Kak district, none of the April 17 women (those living in areas liberated after 1975) was given a job as a nurse.[32]

Young girls between the ages of 12 and 13 left home and volunteered to become medical staff. In the Southwest Zone, Ta Mok's four daughters, one of whom was named Lin, aka Krou, were nurses in the Southwest Zone. Comrade Chea, the secretary of Region 25, kept his daughter with comrade Phea (Ieng Thirith) in a pediatric hospital called P-1. In 1978, Pol Pot said that "health care" was not to be delivered in a capitalist fashion.[33]

The author interviewed a former medical staff named Chea Phal who is now living in former Khmer Rouge strongholds of Anglong Veng. She was originally from Tramkak district, Takeo province. She is now 56 and was married to Chhim Phon, 57, in 1980. They have two children together. Her wedding was arranged by the Khmer Rouge along with five other couples. Today her husband has a crippled right arm after a stray bullet hit it while he was climbing a mountain with fellow soldiers in 1979. It was rotten for a few weeks before he reached a Khmer Rouge hospital. Its radius bone was never reconstructed.[34]

In 1974 Chea Phal left home and joined the revolution after her village chief contacted her family. She was assigned as a messenger for the commune office and then in 1975 as Khmer Rouge medical staff in April 17 Hospital. Her hospital used both modern and traditional

32 Ibid.
33 Searching for the Truth 34.
34 Author's interview with Chea Phal in Anlong Veng district, 30 June 2012.

medicines. Chea Phal knew how to make alcohol and medicines for headache, diarrhea and fever. Alcohol was made from the following ingredients: palm sugar, Rumdeng plant, Chheu Em vine and bamboo leaves. These were put together according to their proportion. Then water was added. The brew was left to ferment for one week. After that the water was boiled. Its steam condensed as alcohol. Chea Phal said she tested whether it was pure alcohol by throwing a spoonful of it into the fire. If it was pure alcohol it would catch flame. Headache medicine was made from cassava flour, lime juice and a chemical component. Diarrhea pill was made from bark of Kantel plant boiled in water according to a proper composition. After one third of the water evaporated through boiling, the remaining water was mixed with cassava flour to make pills. Fever medicine was made from Bandol Pich vine, Sleng nut and water.[35]

Mom Yov did not have immediate care. Norng Chen could not leave the sawmill to care for his wife and thus requested Phal's unit chief to release him from the group to return home to care for his mother. It was an arrangement which suited him well. As a boy Phal could feed his mother water, rice soup and other things around the house which his mother needed. Because there was no modern medicine and adequate intake of food was not available, Mom Yov became more serious. Her body became skinnier while her limbs continued to swell. She could only speak softly when needed Phal's help. She did not want to go to provincial or zonal hospital far away from home. She did not trust medical staff there who she never knew and could treat her harshly. Worst still, they could simply leave her to die in hospital bed.

Norng Chen became creative and sought ways to treat her using wild plants. He had discussed the medicine with members of the cooperative who had some knowledge about the practice. With approval from the cooperative, he collected some tree roots and boiled it for several hours to get concentrated medicinal water which remained about a

---

35 Author's interview with Chea Phal in Anlong Veng district, 30 June 2012.

third of the amount he put in. With luck after drinking this for a week and with continued rest, Mom Yov's condition improved. Her limbs started to heal and she began to walk. Treatment by traditional medicine was never assured. Nobody knew how much water and plant was enough for a patient's condition. It was basic and used as the last resort. The Khmer Rouge encouraged such practice but very few people believed in it. In traditional Khmer society, the medicinal skills are handed down for generations through trials and errors and used sparingly. Still modern medicine is the more measured option.

The Arrest of Phal's Father, Norng Chen

Phal's family was doing well for more than three years into the radical Khmer Rouge's agricultural utopia. Apart from Mom Yov's illness, other family members adapted reasonably well. Phal's brothers and sister also worked well in their various mobile units of adolescents considered to be the spearhead of the revolution. In fact the family's contribution of farm animals were welcome by the cooperative after some criticism of greed and selfishness.

Like all other people during the Khmer Rouge, before this regime ended nobody knew who would live or die. Change could happen at any moment and you never knew for what reasons. For Phal's family, tragedy came in early September 1978. One morning, a group of Khmer Rouge soldiers arrived at the cooperative in a few cars. They were sent from Phnom Penh and headed straight to the sawmill. They did not stop by to discuss with the cooperative chief. Upon arrival at the mill, they handed a letter to Norng Chen who was working with his sweat falling profusely. After reading it and understood the meaning, Norng Chen hurriedly collected his few belongings and boarded one of the vehicles toward Phnom Penh.

Norng Chen did not have the time to inform Mom Yov, his children, his colleagues at the sawmill or anybody. The letter looked important and came from very high up. Nobody else needed consultation and was to be requested information from. Phal's paternal uncle named Chreb who was also working at the sawmill at the time witnessed the unusual assignment with the Khmer Rouge soldiers. He secretly ran to Mom Yov who was staying in the cottage. He gasped and told her: "Sister, my, my brother was taken to Phnom Penh! It did not look good." After informing Phal's mother, he swiftly returned to his duty at the sawmill pretending he had not noticed anything out of order.

Phal's mother took several deep breaths upon hearing the dreaded news. Her hands reached to Phal who was still caring for her at the cottage and his little brother Norng Chen Ly nearby and said, "I don't know what would happen to your father. I am so worried." A neighbor also asked her about Norng Chen, "What happened to sawmill chief Norng Chen? I saw he went with the soldiers." His mother replied, "I have no idea where he went and for what reasons. He did not have the time to tell me about this new assignment." Inside both the neighbor and Phal's mother knew that there was a good chance his father was being accused of some "crimes" and usually people never returned once being taken away.

After Norng Chen was taken away in the direction of Phnom Penh, the workers in the sawmill became apprehensive. They did not know why Norng Chen was arrested and why crimes he committed. Not knowing the truth was the most difficult things to counter for survivors of the Khmer Rouge regime. The Khmer Rouge knew this trick very well. They never informed people about the real facts surrounding them. When people were arrested, they could come in a quiet and gentle manner to eliminate all suspicions and possible resistance from the people. In fact, a few people after being taken away returned home un-harmed. This gave the people a belief that resistance was death while not resisting was survival. The majority who did not resist died in the end. It was the specific result of enforced disappearance practiced in other countries. The workers had no choice but to try their best to achieve results for Angkar at the sawmill. They had to meet and exceed targets set for them to eliminate doubts that they could be next. They dared not talk much to fellow colleagues as well. The informants for Norng Chen's arrest could be among them, passing villagers or village militria (kong chhlob). Nobody knew for sure. The fear of being arrested next filled the air. Inside the workers were also saddened for the loss of Phal's father who had been a kind leader to them as well sacrificed many cattle for Angkar.

Reeducation and Transformation for Love Crime

A month after Norng Chen was taken, there was a commotion. In an afternoon at the sawmill, someone sounded the bell made of spoke of truck wheel so loud as if there was an emergency. Everyone gathered to the meeting hall looking terrified not knowing what would unfold. They were expecting troubles. Mom Yov and Phal were also present in the meeting but they had a sense of hope and unexpectedness because in a meeting like that news about Norng Chen could be revealed. A well-built man with dark complexion walked into the meeting. He announced short and clear in front of a few hundred people that "there is a moral offense in our cooperative."

Phal heard it but he did not really understand what it meant. He yanked his mother's sleeves and asked: "What does it mean by moral offense?" His mother replied, "Shush, I don't know yet, just wait and listen son. Stay still." The dark man who announced it made people standing in a circle about 20 meter in diameter. Then he summoned a man and a woman to the middle. He then said, "These two are in a romantic relationship; they met each other during working hours without permission from Angkar." Phal knew the two adult persons very well. The man was a "new people" who had been transferred from Phnom Penh, while the woman was a "base people" who had lived in the village since before the Khmer Rouge regime arrived. They were accused by Angkar of committing "love crime" because they met without the approval or prior arrangement by Angkar. In Angkar's new rule, they had to be arranged in marriages with tens more couples. Angkar would choose for them their appropriate lovers. Only then they could live with each other or meet occasionally after assignments to make children for Angkar.

For the couple in question, they had to be "reeducated and transformed." After the meeting, the two were escorted by several village militia away from the village. Three days later Phal noticed the man's scarf on one of the militiamen. A few weeks later further news came to light that the man had been executed. In the Khmer Rouge regime, "reeducation and transformation" meant execution. It was harsh and the Khmer Rouge intended it to be loud and clear to everyone participating in the meeting that secret love was strictly forbidden by Angkar. Still the regime was not perfect. No amount of harsh control and killing could monitor everyone in the country. Among Khmer Rouge cadres themselves, there were reports of love affairs in certain villages.

Some arranged couples however remained together long after the Khmer Rouge regime was overthrown. By chance the people with the right chemistry were chosen for each other and were able to build a family afterwards. In Khmer traditional society in pre-Democratic Kampuchea period, most marriages were arranged by parents or guardians who judged potential partners based on family history, personal behavior, achievements, occupation and education. Mostly teachers and doctors were preferred. In the Khmer Rouge time, the arranged marriages were based on revolutionary zeal and achievements under Angkar. But the most difficult situation the bride or the groom found it easy to accept was couples with complete contrast in socioeconomic background, age, personal preferences or religious orientations. The Khmer society did not condone racism or prejudices but once it came to personal relationship, parents and couples became specific about the special persons they wanted their children or themselves to live with. Some Khmer Rouge marriages broke up as soon as the regime collapsed. The percentage of lasting relationship as opposed to broke ones arranged by the Khmer Rouge is not yet known.

The Khmer Rouge Arrested Mom Yov

A few months after the summon of Phal's father,[36] the Khmer Rouge militiamen came to find Phal's mother. Phal was still staying with his mother along with his youngest brother Norng Chen Ly. The Khmer Rouge took them together. They lied them that they wanted to take them to meet Norng Chen in Phnom Penh. Upon hearing that and seeing the opportunity to ride a truck, Phal was excited. In Phnom Penh, he imagined, he would meet his father, see the bustling city with its fills of trucks, motorbikes and tricycles. He also wanted his beloved grounded ice cone with sweetened coconut milk which he had missed since leaving his village in Kampot. Phal also wanted to see the Royal Palace, the grand independence monument and Wat Phnom which are the attractions in the city often talked about by elders and young people in his village. The sight and sound of the city was fascinating.

In the heat of Cambodia's tropical weather, ice was a miracle. In pre-Khmer Rouge time, it was not widely produced in Cambodia. A block of ice was an amazing sight for Phal which he had seen only once before. He had heard that Phnom Penh was filled with ice in all shops. Phal's young imagination ran wild upon hearing the discussion about going to the city and meet his lost father. Phal was really looking forward to it.

Without asking for clarification from the Khmer Rouge, Mom Yov hurriedly gathered her belongings, but the Khmer Rouge lied her again by saying, "Do not take much with you. You will go only for two

---

36 It is important to note that both Norng Chen and Mom Yov arrived at S-21 at about nine days apart, according to their biographies recorded at S-21. However, Norng Chan Phal remembered his father had been taken a few months before December 1978. It was possible that Norng Chen was incarcerated somewhere else before finally taken to S-21.

nights." Mom Yov reflected that two nights might be enough because Kampong Speu was not that far from the city. Then she left her cottage with her two sons taking only a few basic possessions as they did not have much anyway. Under Angkar, no private properties were allowed beside the most basic tools for sleeping, clothing and eating. Phal remembered that he also left behind a female cat and its three kittens.

Mom Yov, Phal and his younger brother Ly walked up several village paths toward the national road 4 where they saw a Jeep awaiting them. Two Khmer Rouge soldiers armed with AK-47s looking bored and angry were waiting beside the car. Two women were already there. One woman was holding the hand of her two-year old son and carrying a six-month old baby girl. The other woman was holding a four-month old baby boy. Together they boarded the Jeep and travelled east toward Phnom Penh. Mom Yov looked at the women who returned the gaze but the women did not talk to each other. Travelling with soldiers was unusual especially when being board a car. Something urgent must have needed their attention. The road was bumpy on some spots due to heavy use without maintenance and landmine explosions during the fighting. As it got closer to Phnom Penh the ride was smooth and quiet. Neither the Khmer Rouge nor the women uttered a word. Nobody was allowed to talk; none trusted each other.

A two hours later they arrived the outskirt of town. Phal noticed that along the road there were virtually no people. The situation was too eerily quiet for a capital city. It was quieter than Kampot town which Phal had visited a few years ago with his father. New and old vehicles, perhaps damaged, were left by the side of the road which was littered with uncollected trash. It was a scene of neglect in which a large number of people had been there but left soon afterward, just like a concert field completed overnight. Once a while Phal saw lone Khmer Rouge soldier standing guard, providing security on the road.

Despite the unusual sight, Phal was still excited. He would not let go of excitement. After all the world was full of unexpectedness for a young boy like Phal who by then was already 8 years old. Maybe Phnom Penh city center was different, Phal thought. Maybe people no longer lived in the outskirt anymore. Still he needed confirmation from his mother. He found his mother's hand and asked, "Are we there yet Mum?" Mom Yov smiled a little and tapped her head without saying much. She was also lost in her own thought and imagination for the unexpected. His mother knew best what was going to happen but she did not say it. The Khmer Rouge soldiers were on the car as well so there was little time to explain little Phal about her observation. She turned and looked ahead. The incoming wind blew her hair gently as the Jeep drove slowly into town center.

Mom Yov's little grin gave Phal a slight confirmation that his father was awaiting them and the he would meet him soon. He then continued observing the side of the road and the objects left behind along the way in the empty outskirt. As the car got closer the same emptiness continued. Silence persisted. Grass and small trees grew through the crack of the roads along the city's major boulevards as if no one had been using it for some time. There were many beautiful houses; some with doors opened, others with doors closed, but were not inhabited. By then it got strange even to the young observer like Phal. It was his first time visiting Phnom Penh, the capital city of Cambodia and it was the first time the city was abandoned and inhabited since it was founded a few hundred years ago. For Phal it was a rare privilege but it was the beginning of his ordeal as a boy witnessing the tragedy that would befall his family and suffering the consequences of it along with his other siblings.

Arriving the Train Station

Phnom Penh has just one train station built during the Sangkum Reastr Niyum period under Prince Norodom Sihanouk's tutelage. From the station, Phnom Penh was connected to the coast as well as to the border with Thailand. The railway was intended to be the artery of Cambodia's trade with the world and highway to Southeast Asia.

The Jeep continued taking Phal steadily into the city. It passed tall and impressive university buildings as it got closer to town center. Phal had hope to meet his father that day. The jeep made a few left turns and finally came to a stop at the train station, only one kilometer from the former and empty French embassy. The Khmer Rouge driver got off the Jeep and immediately told them to stay for three days at the station. The women had to find a place within the station to camp and wait for further instruction from Angkar. The driver left with a few Khmer Rouge soldiers. Only one remained. They thought that for three women and five children there was not any need for more guards. He was armed with AK-47 and remained with them at all time. He said just a few words to the women and that they must not wander outside the station perimeter.

When being arrested, Mom Yov was not fully recovered from her illness. She was still on traditional medication. When taken to Phnom Penh she also brought along her medicine. A day after staying at the train station, Mom Yov medicinal water ran out and her condition worsened. Perhaps it was worry about her life and the fate of her husband and children. Perhaps she really needed more attention. She requested the Khmer Rouge to start a fire to boil plants which she brought along. Normally she would boil the medicine and keep only a third of the water after evaporation through the boiling process. She would drink that water. The soldier denied her permission and said, "No fire is allowed here; the fire will damage the station floor." But when she asked to do it outside he did not allow too. He was afraid that she would run away. The women and children were provided only one meal per day between 12 pm and 1 pm. Mom Yov would eat only a few spoons and gave the rest to Phal and his little brother.

On the third day, Phal became anxious for not seeing his father and for lack of activities at the train station. For all his expectation about Phnom Penh, it did not deliver. He was restricted to spaces inside the train station. Phal began asking his mother, "Mother, they said father was sent to work here and why have we not met him now?" She did not answer. Still weak from her recurring illness and with worry herself, Mom Yov did not have the strength to explain Phal. Phal became insistent. He repeated the question to her many times. Eventually Mom Yov approached the soldier and asked, "Do you know a man named Norng Chen? He was sent from Kampong Speu to here?" The Khmer Rouge replied, "There is no answer for your question. Do not try to play trick with me." Mom Yov was shocked as she had been told to come here to see her husband and were not supposed to be treated like prisoners.

3. THE TERROR OF S-21

In the afternoon of the fourth day at around 3:30 pm, the Khmer Rouge soldiers coming on the same Jeep arrived the train station. They boarded the women and children on the car and began driving to the south side the city, again through the quiet street of the usually bustling capital. After four days of inactivity, Phal was relieved to see the city again albeit the emptiness of it. The paved roads and the houses with occasional taller buildings lining the streets were a different sight to what he had seen in the village. Then his thought about the whereabouts and the logics of being taken and moved around returned. Phal through, "Where are the Khmer Rouge soldiers taking us to? We already arrived the train station three days ago and it was where father was supposed to work." Phal kept the hope that his father would emerge somewhere at the end of the ride to greet him and his mother.

As he was enjoying the ride, the Jeep stopped at a place with barbed wire fence with three meter tin wall. The Jeep stopped at a corrugated gate leading to the compound. Without notification, the gate swung open by guards inside the compound. Phal saw six Khmer Rouge soldiers in black clothes standing on both sides of the entrance looking at him and the women in grimed faces. As the first people to greet them, Phal tried to look at the faces hoping that one of them would be his father's. His father could have been waiting here to welcome him. Nobody knew. The Khmer Rouge regime was full of unpredictability. But after scanning all the face, his was not among them. Even if he was with them, he wouldn't have let him scanning his face. He would have approached Phal and carry him off the jeep.

The Front Gate

He was not at the train station and now he was nowhere to be found. Suddenly the six vile Khmer Rouge soldiers approached the car in a manner that was much worse than the soldier who guarded them at the station. They shouted wildly at the women to immediately get off the Jeep. Worse still the driver who had been in a benign manner toward them suddenly became a different person. He also shouted and pushed them, women and children, to get off the Jeep. Phal had nowhere for help or someone to explain the situation. He gazed at his mother. He could see that Mom Yov was bewildered and afraid. His dream of seeing his father began to fate. It was not the treatment he had hoped. His father would not be in this place.

Shaken, the women complied slowly as they struggled to comprehend the plight that befell them. Because Mom Yov had illness which caused her limbs to swell and was tired from the trip, she was slower than others to react to order and the situation. The Khmer Rouge threw her from the Jeep onto the ground. She struggled to get up with her clothes smeared with dirt. She also carefully pick up the medicine jar she brought along. But the Khmer Rouge yanked the medicine jar and threw it on the street. His mother ran to collect the jar but then the Khmer Rouge beat her and stomped her as she lower down to take the jar and its spilled contents from the ground. It was her one hope to treat her swollen illness wherever she went. Phal could barely witness it but he could do nothing to help his mother from this torture. Her hands reached him and his brother as she began to walk inside the compound and toward a registration room. Mom Yov and the women were brought to the notorious S-21 security center which the Khmer Rouge used to detain, torture and kill alleged enemies of Angkar.

The Cruelty in Registration Room

The Khmer Rouge pushed and kicked Mom Yov into the first room of the prison which was the registration room without concern for her humanity, dignity or frailty. When inside the room, they measured her body height. They sat her on a chair with her back posturing straight up with her head leaning on an iron meter. Then the Khmer Rouge took her photograph. Because Mom Yov was a country woman and did not get used to being photographed she did not satisfy the regis- tration staff's composure demand. The photographer grabbed her hair and pull her back and forth, left and right until she satisfied their de- mand. He also slapped her faces several times demanding her to do exactly what he wanted. As he did that he used insulting and cursing words toward her as if she had made serious mistakes. Phal stood there witnessing the cruelty toward his beloved mother and unable to help her. He was stunned and also afraid for himself. No amount of cru- elty he had witnessed in Kampong Speu could closely compare with what he was seeing toward his mother. Phal was spared the treatment. His photograph was not taken. His biography was not written in the log book. After Mom Yov was done with the photograph, the Khmer Rouge measured and photographed the other two women.

After taking her picture, the Khmer Rouge dragged Mom Yov further to a nearby room where they asked her many strange questions. Phal followed with his younger brother. Mom Yov could not understand questions or was not able to find fitting answers. She answered them wrongly several times. Coming from Kampot, she had a distinct ac- cent which the Khmer Rouge did not understand fully. The questions posed were also political, technical and related to spying and collab- oration. As it went on the Khmer Rouge became more enraged and kicked her to the ground. Her nose and mouth bled profusely. Phal and his brother rushed to hug her legs as they cried.

After the beating, the Khmer Rouge ordered Mom Yov to clean the tile floor of her blood. She took out her scarf to do it as her hands trem- bled. In her heart she knew she and her children were in grave danger. Norng Chen had perhaps been executed. As Phal tried to lift his moth- er after she cleaned the floor, the Khmer Rouge stepped on his fingers with their hard tire shoes causing them to bleed like water but he did not feel the pain. Phal only remembers the incident and the blood but he did not remember crying from it. The fear and the sympathy for his mother had numbed it. Up till that point his mother and father had worked so hard for Angkar. They had donated their cattle and elephant for Angkar in the sawmill. Their children including Phal were scattered in different units to work days and nights for Angkar. Still they were brought to S-21 and his mother was treated like a criminal. His father was nowhere to be seen. Two other women who were carrying their babies entering the prison on the same day were treated as badly.

The Last Night with His Mother

After taking photograph, the Khmer Rouge brought his mother to the third building of the S-21. The prison was a converted school with four main buildings on the edges and a central administrative building in the middle. The third building was surrounded with barbed wire to prevent prisoners from escaping. The guards put Phal's mother and the other two women in room number two which was a common room for many prisoners. This room was reserved for least important prisoners. Then the Khmer Rouge shackled his mother with two rudimentary iron hooks with a single iron bar which ran through the hooks of other prisoners in the room. They then closed the door after having done this. Phal and his brother stayed with Mom Yov through the night. She found enough space on the bare floor to lay her right arm for Phal and his younger brother to sleep on. Her left arm held the blooded scarf which she used to swat away mosquitos from biting her two sons. Mom Yov kept crying through the night fearing for the safety of herself and her sons. Witnessing the deteriorating situation, Phal tried to ask her: "Mother, why father is not here to help us? Why did they beat you? What is this place? Why are we here? What is the iron on your ankles for? The stench in this room is unbearable mother." As a boy Phal did not know anything about the suffering his mother was going through. He could only have deep sympathy for her now.

When he asked her too much, his mother closed his mouth and told him, "Do not talk, they could hear us and will beat you and me again." Phal then tried to sleep but was awakened occasionally due to noise of other prisoners moaning with pain and the iron hooks and bar clashing each other as the legs were moved. His mother continued to swat mosquitos from biting him for the whole night as she pondered their fates. Soon the groans and the stench overcame his curiosity. He became restless but he no longer wanted to ask his mother about what was happening to them besides a longing to get out of this place as soon as possible.

The treatment on prisoner by the guards, interrogators and staff of S-21 was harsh as is shown in the prison's regulations for prisoners below.

Basic regulations at S-21 read:

1. You must answer according to my questions. Do not turn them away.
2. Do not try to hide the facts by making pretexts of this and that. You are strictly prohibited to contest me.
3. Do not be a fool for you are someone who dares to thwart the revolution.
4. You must immediately answer my questions without wasting time to reflect.
5. Do not tell me either about your immoralities or the revolution.
6. While getting lashes or electric shocks, you must not cry out at all.
7. Do nothing. Sit still and wait for my orders. If there are no orders, keep quiet. When I ask you to do something, you must do it right away without protesting.
8. Do not make pretexts about Kampuchea Krom so as to hide your true existence as a traitor.
9. If you do not follow all the above rules, you shall get many lashes or electric shocks.
10. If you disobey any point of my regulations, you shall get either ten lashes or five electric shocks.[37]

---

37 DC-Cam archives.

Mom Yov's Last Words

In the early morning, the sun rays began piecing through the louver windows of the room which had been built as a classroom. Three guards unlocked and opened the doors. They then shouted, "All children must go downstairs." Mom Yov suddenly grabbed his arm and whispered to Phal's ear, "Look after your younger brother my son!" After that she reached out into her deep pocket and handed Phal a small packet of ointment for him to apply on mosquito bite spots. There was not much left in the packet but mother handed to me anyway. Mother was pushed against the window for trying to grab Phal's hands. The Khmer Rouge yanked the hands of Phal and brother and took them out of the room leaving Mom Yov shackled alone with concern for her children. They also took away a toddler and two babies from the two women who shared the trip with Phal. Mothers and babies cried loudly as they struggled to hold onto each other. The mothers demanded to keep her babies because they did not stop breastfeeding. Because their ankles were locked by the shackles, they could not resist the guards' forceful pull. Upon having the babies, the guards kicked and stomped one of the mothers to the floor until she lost consciousness. The guards then quickly locked the room with Phal, his brother, a toddler and two babies in their hands. Mom Yov tried to look at him through the window slates until the guards walked past to the ground floor. One guard held Phal's and his brother's hands. The other two held the hand of a toddler and carried a baby each. Because Phal was slow. He was pushed down the stairs it approached the ground. Phal stumbled and cried. The guard then told him, cried he said, "Stop crying or I'll beat you up like your mother." They brought him through an iron gate at the back of the prison compound.

Inmate Workshop and Prison Kitchen

Behind buildings two and three, the Khmer Rouge used an old barn with brief wall as a workshop for inmates who had special skills to create furniture, sculptures and repair equipment for the prison. Next to this workshop was a kitchen where food was prepared for prisoners. The guards dropped the children in the kitchen. They sat them down on bare dirt floor and put the babies onto a pile of old clothes which were accumulated by incoming prisoners' belongs. Then they told an old woman who was cooking food for prisoners to look after the children and to not let them stray inside the prison compound. The guards then opened the gate and reentered the compound. The cook stared at Phal who was the oldest and said, "Stay still and do not go anywhere, otherwise you will be beaten." Having finished her warning, the woman went back to cooking diligently. She did not have anyone to talk to and concentrated on her task at hand.

After the guards were gone and the woman became intense in her cooking, Phal began exploring the workshop and the kitchen. He saw three old men working in the workshop bending iron polls to make shackle rings for locking prisoners. They were focused on their work as well with little talk between them. Neither did they border to talk to Phal or play with the babies. These people were also prisoners just like Phal's mother and were afraid that any talking or a simple mistake could get them killed.

Phal continued looking. He saw two large cooking pans filled with what looked like food for pigs or other animals. Next to these pans was a large pile of old clothes of about two to three meter high where they babies were placed. Further from the pile was a pig cage with several pigs inside. A pile of old furniture was laid near the workshop. It was perhaps for the workmen to complete.

Having finished observing the surroundings, Phal heard the stream of prisoners coming from building number one on the south side of the prison. Perhaps they were being tortured in some ways. He tried gleaning through the fence with a view between buildings two and three. He saw emaciated prisoners, men, women and young adults being brought out from the prison through the front gate. Some were naked, others were tied. The skinniest prisoners were allowed to walk without being tied. Their hair almost stood still due to lack of shower for many days or weeks. Their faces were blank, no hope, no energy, no resistance as if they were ready to receive their final fate. Some slow walking prisoners were whipped with electric wire. The scene horrified Phal who had heard about Khmer Rouge cruelty back in the village but never saw it with his own eyes. The sight of these prisoners made Phal think about his mother's condition and future inside building three. Although Phal used to be very active, he remained with his brother near the pile of clothes with the toddler and two babies.

Last Sight of His Mother

At around 12 pm on the same day, Phal's younger brother who was about six years old at the time and the kids started crying because of hunger and thirst. His brother asked Phal to bring him to their mother who was being locked in building three of the prison. He asked Phal again and again to bring him water and to take him to see their mother. Phal could not resist him any longer. Phal started thinking about ways to satisfy this needs. As he looked up the building three, unexpectedly through the window Phal saw his mother somehow looking straight down at him, her hands holding window bars. The window was open that day; normally all windows were closed. She looked concerned for the safety of her children. Mom Yov loved her kids and even in the direst situation she also placed their wellbeing on top of her priorities. Now that she was locked in place, her children were kept in the hands of coldblooded Khmer Rouge torturers.

As Phal stared at his mother, his younger brother followed his line of sight. He saw his mother and cried even harder demanding to go upstairs to see her. Seeing them looking at her and her kid crying for her, she began to cry. She made a hand gesture to Phal to calm down his brother as his cry could alert the Khmer Rouge guards who would come and beat them or worse they could simply silence them forever by smashing them in some tree trunks or hard poles which witnesses saw them doing against children.

Heeding his mother's advice, Phal tried to trick his brother to stop crying. He comforted him, "Please stop crying brother, mother will come down soon. If you don't stop angry guard will come to take you." Hearing that he did stop. Phal bended down to wipe his tears from his checks and tab his back. He felt more assured. He then looked up to tell his mother of what I did. She disappeared. He tried to look at another window. She was not there. Phal has not seen his mother since. He later learnt that on that day she was brought to an interrogation room and later executed at Cheung Ek killing fields about 15 kilometers from S-21 prison.

Soothing Crying Babies

The babies who were placed on the pile of clothes began crying as well. They cried until they could not make any more sound. Seeing this the old cook walked to them with a bowl of porridge from one of the giant cooking pans and said to Phal, "Feed them with this, they will stop crying." Phal did exactly that. One baby was about six months old, so he could eat the porridge. The other one was just four months old who could not eat but drink the soup from the porridge. After feeding them, the kids were still hungry and Phal only took a few spoons from it. Phal approached the cook and asked for some more, "Can I have some more aunty?" She replied quickly, "No you can't, for the four of you there is only one bowl. The rest will go to the prisoners upstairs. If the porridge is not enough, I will be punished for it." Upon saying that she returned to work quietly intending her communication with Phal to be as limited as possible. The cook and the men working here were also prisoners with specific skills which the Khmer Rouge used temporarily.

Several meters away from the cooking area, just around the place where rainwater would fall from the roof, Phal found a few pieces of broken jars which contained some water. He used the porridge bowl which he had not returned to the cook to scoop some water to drink and to feed the two babies. The water was filled with mosquito lavas and it smelled but it was the only water he had. The water tasted sour and bitter at the same time. That day all five of them had diarrhea throughout the night.

Emergency Evacuation of S-21

At around 8 am of the third day, the woman cook who was tasked to look after the children went out to all the buildings to collect dishes after serving the prisoners with food the day before. She came back with hurried face and left the dishes to one side of the kitchen. She began looking around at the commotion inside the prison compound. The guards ran around from cells to cells, and called out to each other loudly that "the Vietnamese are approaching the city, bring all the prisoners out from the prison cells. There is not much time." Phal saw them tying up prisoners with the hands to the back. They blindfolded some prisoners, while other prisoners were unclothed. Some female prisoners wore tone clothes and their bodies resembled skeletons with skin covering it. They must have been in the cells for a long time.

The guards pushed and kicked the prisoners ordering them to walk faster toward the front gate where trucks were waiting for them. But some blindfolded prisoners stumbled causing the other prisoners to fall as well because they were tied together with a long robe. This delayed the evacuation further. As they struggled to get up with their arms bound to the back, the Khmer Rouge scolded at them. Once they stood up they walked blindly to different directions. The guards became even more enraged. They beat some and threatened the others. A guard took out a bamboo pole the size of an adult wrist and struck at the heads of some prisoners. It sounded like one was hitting a baseball bat against coconut shells. The strike caused the prisoners to bleed from the head profusely and the blood dripped on the shoulders and onto the bodies. The scene was terrifying. Phal wanted to run away and hide in the kitchen with his brother and the babies but he had to continue looking intensely skipping the barbarity and searching for resemblance of his parents. Because it was too far, most prisoners were blindfolded and there were too many zombie figures, he could not find his parents. Almost all prisoners were evacuated from the prison through the front gate that day.

Hiding in the Clothes

As he was looking at the evacuation, he began realizing that the five children including him were also prisoners which meant they were the subject of evacuation as well. This realization shook his knees. The guards communicated with each other, "Are all the prisoners evacuated?" A guard replied that almost all the prisoners were evacuated. Another loud voice coming from building three noted that "do not forget the children in the kitchen." As he heard that Phal was terrified. All his senses became focused for solutions on the safety of himself, his younger brother and the two babies. His mother told him to look after his brother. So he could not run away without him. He did not want to leave the babies behind as well. He also thought that if his mother was still alive, she could come to collect them in the kitchen. So changing positions by running away was not ideal. Plus he did not know the environment around the prison. He did not have a place to run to.

As he was contemplating his escape plan, he found the pile of prisoner clothes. The workers and the cook were not there. He waited until the guards were too busy within the prison compound. Then he collected the toddler and the two babies along with his brother and burrowed them into the pile of clothes. The clothes were both wet and stinky. He also felt the sensation of itch on his body although throughout the Khmer Rouge time he had not had proper clothes to wear and his body had been exposed all the time. This cloth pile was much dirtier than what he had experienced before. To hide he need to stay hidden within it. So it was suffocating at the same time. The two babies tried to cry but they could not gather the strength to do so as they were starved of food and breast milk from their mothers for a few days. They only sounded a little. The clothes also helped muffling their cries.

A moment later the woman cook and a few guards did come looking for them. They did not really search. They were fearing for their safety and did not have enough time to escape. A guard walked close to the pile and asked, "Where have they gone?" Another guard replied, "Maybe other guards collected them already." The woman cook joined in, "I don't think so. I just left them in the kitchen a short moment ago before I went into one of the prison cells. No other guards should have come here." A guard replied, "We must find them quickly. The Vietnamese soldiers are approaching Phnom Penh. We do not have much time." After looking here and there hastily, they simply left. It was a huge relief for Phal and his action saved them just in time. He tried to cover the mouth of his brother and restricted his movement within the pile. Luckily the babies had stopped crying and remained also still.

Silence

After the guards left the workshop, Phal felt an incomparable happiness and a sense of new life awaited me. Phal thought that he would be able to meet his parents, his elder siblings and friends in Kampong Speu province when he returned. At around 2 to 3 pm, it was quiet. He peered through the clothes into the prison compound and found nobody walking around as usual. The gates were left open. He did not know for sure if all the guards had left. He continued lying in the clothes waiting for his parents to come find him. If he left, they would not be able to find him when they returned to the prison. Also walking around in prison could get him killed at the hands of the ruthless prison guards who might stay behind.

The kids began crying and told Phal they wanted to drink water and eat food. His younger brother constantly asked for his mother. The babies were incessantly crying as they needed breast milk. Phal began searching for answers to comfort the babies as well as to convince his younger brother to remain calm amid thirst and hunger. He told him that the guard would come to take him and hurt him if he continued crying loudly. As for the babies there was no way to stop them. The lack of breast milk sapped heir energy and their cries became quieter as the hours went by.

Falling Artillery Shells

At around 5 pm the same day, Phal became terrified yet again after hearing canon shells landing in the distance and started creeping closer and closer toward the prison compound. The thunderous sound of exploding shells shook everything nearby. The children were so terrified that they forgot about the hunger and cuddled together under the clothes. If a shell landed nearby they would not be protected but the cloth cover provided them a sense of safety and concealment. Phal's only hope was that his mother would pick him up at some point, but he did not know when she could come. He did not sleep for the whole night.

The clothes offered also protection against mosquito bites. It was better than the night he spent with his mother in the cell. In the fourth morning, the sound of shelling disappeared. Only a few sporadic gun fights were heard. His younger brother kept asking him for their mother, "I am hungry; I need to see mother. Why is it taking her so long to find us here?" Phal replied, "Stay here I go look for her." He nodded. Phal began creeping from inside the clothes and walked toward the unlocked prison gate next to the workshop. His eyes scanned for any remaining prison guards who might be left behind. He walked slowly toward building three where his mother had been imprisoned. When he reached her cell in the upper floor, he found an unlocked door with empty cell. The shackles which were used to lock her were left in place but all prisoners were removed. He began searching in other buildings. Because it seemed empty, he tried calling her. If she was hiding somewhere she could come to him as she recognized his voice. No one heard him. Not a single person remained at the prison.

Discovering Corpses

Phal continued to search the empty prison. When he arrived at building one, he saw several bodies lying on the prison's iron beds. From a distance the body appeared to be sleeping people lying flatly on the bed with one of their ankles locked up to the bed frame. Phal noticed strange fishy smell coming out of the room with lots of flies buzzing in and out of the rooms. The bodies appeared lifeless. One thing was certain, the bodies appeared to be prisoners not guards. So Phal felt assured and comfortable enough to get closer to check for information of his parents. Maybe the prisoners knew. As he did that he saw the bodies covered with blood dripping onto the Khmer tile floor. It was a terrifying sight. Phal had never seen corpses before. The prisoners had been executed by incision on the throats only hours ago, perhaps during the evacuation. Nobody knew why these men were not taken away like the others. He quickly returned to the workshop where his brother wasted no time to ask, "Did you find mother?" Phal told him, "No mother is not here. I found several bodies which had been killed very recently. Phal's brother continued crying. He appeared to have given hope of seeing their parents, at least for the medium term.

Phal did not know the surroundings and so he remained in the workshop. During the night he stayed in the clothes. During the day he foraged for any remaining food and water in the kitchen. He found in one of the large cooking pans some porridge. The children fed on that until it became spoiled. Then Phal found some food in another covered pan which the cook had made for the pigs. They ate that as well. The pig food allowed them to quench some hunger and endured the ordeal until help arrived, if it ever came. Even for a child like Phal, sense of hope was lingering. The end of the cruelty and his misery was near.

Liberation

The next day, Phal and the children saw soldiers approaching the prison compound. They hurriedly returned to the clothes to hide. They lost sight of them afterward. As they were looking from inside the clothes, two Vietnamese soldiers appeared in front of them. One of them spoke broken Khmer language. He asked, "Come out now. We saw you burrowing in there. Are you Khmer Rouge children? Are you Pol Pot's children?" It took Phal a while to register the situation and comprehend the shocked arrival of the Vietnamese soldiers. Phal gathered his voice to reply, "My father is Norng Chen and my mother is Mom Yov. We were arrested by the Khmer Rouge and brought here. After recognizing their pale skins due to lack of food and water and insect bites, the Vietnamese soldiers produced a packet of dried cooked rice from one of his army pockets. They then walked to the kitchen and cooked the rice using a small pan which the cook left behind. After feeding them, the two Vietnamese soldiers left. Phal tried to keep some rice for later time as he continued waiting for his parents. The two babies could not eat rice. He could only feed them water.

On the tenth day which was 10 January 1979, Phal woke up on the clothes. Everyone was there. His brother was sleeping. He found the youngest baby of about 4 months old not moving. His body was cold and stiff. He saw some ants crawling up his nostrils. He felt his breath and tried to wake him up but he was unresponsive. He did not know whether he was dead or alive. He tried swatting and plucking away the aunts with his hands and wash him with some wet cloth.

At around 1 am at night, Vietnamese and Cambodian soldiers belonging to the Vietnamese volunteer army and the National United Salvation Armed Forces of Kampuchea entered the prison compound with guns and flashlights. They found the children sleeping in the clothes. They were Phal's ultimate saviors. The soldiers picked up the children from the clothes. One of them took out two army bottles of water from his waist and fed them. Because the children's clothes were partly torn as well as smelly due to lack of shower and prolonged sleeping in dirty prison clothes the soldiers undressed them. They also found extra water to show them that night.

The four month old baby which Phal found stiff during the day was indeed dead. The soldiers buried him near the workshop. The other baby of about six months old was also fading fast but not yet dead. He was lucky and saved. Because the children were frail due to lack of food and water for several days and not much nutrition before that, the soldiers attempted to bring them out of the prison at once, sought some treatment and put them in a shelter outside. Phal told them to keep him in prison because he was waiting for his parents to come. Phal said, "My parents will be coming soon." They told him, "No, you all do not look good. We have to take you out." Having said that they hurriedly carried the children toward a truck outside. Half an hour later, they arrived at an army hospital.

At hospital Phal found so many patients. Some were sick. Others were wounded because of fighting. The doctors and nurses of Vietnamese and Cambodian nationalities were busy giving help and treating the patients. After a while, a doctor approached Phal. He showered the children again, conducted superficial analysis of their health. He gave an I.V. fluid injection with medicine. They fed and clothed the children afterward.

Naming the Baby

The six month old baby recovered very quickly each day. After a week he looked strong and happy. Because Phal did not remember his name. No one at the hospital knew it as well. So the soldiers gave him a named called "Bram Pi Makara" or simply Makara. It meant January 7. It was the official day when Phnom Penh was liberated from the genocidal Khmer Rouge regime and the day chosen for countrywide liberation. Phal remained deeply grateful for the Cambodian and Vietnamese armies for sacrificing their lives in driving away the Khmer Rouge and more specifically rescuing him from the notorious Tuol Sleng prison where up to 14,000 people were tortured and killed.

Without their parents or immediate known relatives, the children moved to many locations with the armies. The soldiers taught them many things including polite talking, eating properly with spoon and chopsticks. They also taught them how to protect ourselves in case of emergency such as shelling and being caught in a firefight. The four surviving children who were found by the Vietnamese and Cambodian soldiers on January 10, 1979 were:

1. Norng Chan Phal, 9 years old
2. Norng Chan Ly, 6 years old
3. Socheat (full name unknown), 2 years old
4. Makara (full name unknown), 6 month old

The Children As They Were Found[38]

---

38 DC-Cam archives.

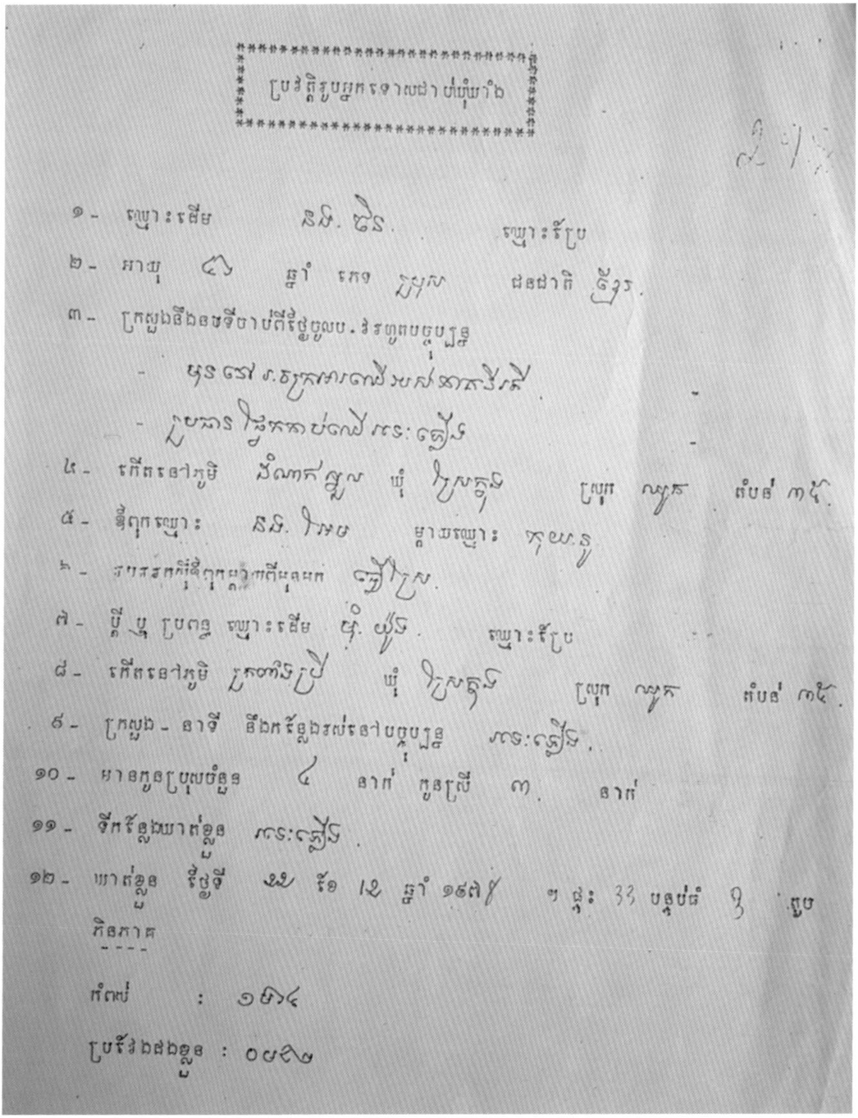

40 Toul Sleng Archives, TSL6245.

4. NEW LIFE

Phal was loved by the soldiers. They taught us proper manners. As a village child, manner was not the things that he had learnt growing up to that point. Gradually Phal was able to speak politely. He also learnt some Vietnamese language from the Vietnamese soldiers. All the rescued children felt loved.

Approximately three months later, news of their incredible and sympathetic survival reached Lork Ta (grandfather)[41] Keo Chenda who was then Phnom Penh governor as well as minister of propaganda. He visited Phal at the shelter in Chamkar Daung village, Roluos commune, Dangkao district, Phnom Penh, about 14 Kilometer from city center. His shelter was not far from Cheung Ek killing fields where his parents were supposed to be transported from S-21 in the city to be executed.

The shelter was the place where he lived with Vietnamese soldiers. Lork Ta Keo Chenda went there to request permission to grant him custody of the rescued children. At first instance the Vietnamese soldiers having built some affectionate connection with the children denied him. But Lork Ta Keo Chenda persisted. He came several times to make the same request. On one occasion, the soldiers told Phal to go hiding so that he would not be able to see him. A week later, he came again and saw Phal playing.

Naturally Phal did not want to go with Lork Ta Keo Chenda because he was happy with the soldiers who had been treating him like their own children, with love and care his own parents had given him. It was something that was completely denied during the Khmer Rouge especially during his brief time in Tuol Sleng prison. Phal cried so hard as he left the soldiers along with his younger brother Norng Chan

---

41 In Khmer word, grandfather was used to call respectable elderly man in the community.

Ly. But it was perhaps a better solution. The soldiers would be moving on from one dangerous location to the next and their positions were not ideal for children.

Phal boarded a small light green Soviet-made car with Lork Ta Keo Chenda back to Phnom Penh. After half an hour he arrived his home. He was greeted by smiling members of Lork Ta Keo Chenda's family. Seeing this Phal was excited. A memory of Khmer Rouge reception at S-21 still lingered in his mind when arriving a new place. Family members gave him candy and home baked cakes. Most importantly they gave him his beloved ground ice with sugar water which he had hoped to taste since Phal was in Kampong Speu. Life was safe and secured. The only thing left in his mind was the fate of his parents and siblings who did not come to meet him. Phal did not know whether they were dead or alive.

As for Norng Chan Ly his longing for his mother did not go away. He normally woke up from his sleep in the middle of the nights asking for his mother. Norng Chan Ly at a young age was still looking for his mother. The cry disturbed the sleep of their new family. Lork Ta Keo Chenda found a babysitter who was a 40-year-old widowed woman whose husband was murdered by the Khmer Rouge. She also had two children.

Growing Up

In 1980, schools throughout the country commenced the new school year. Lork Ta Keo Chenda took Phal to register at Wat Koh elementary school located near his house. Since the country was just liberated, the number of teachers, who were knowledgeable, was small; almost all of them were killed in Democratic Kampuchea. Those who knew more taught those who knew less and those who knew less taught those who knew nothing. One teacher had to teach many students. The majority of students was not healthy. They were sick and less intelligent. It was reconstruction of Cambodia with all available means. The Khmer Rouge had killed most of Cambodia's intellectuals, doctors, teachers and professors. They also destroyed much of the nation's properties and modern equipment making it extremely difficult to re-build the country. Unlike in other post-conflict country, the destruction of Khmer Rouge genocide was highly selective in a manner which brought Cambodia's development backward for a few decades due to population destruction as well as socio-economic and cultural infra-structure. Many women were left as widows. Children were orphaned. Head monks were killed. Religious leaders perished. A large number of population left Cambodia to rebuild a new life in a foreign country by going through the border camps between Cambodia and Thailand.

Family Tracing

In the first post-genocide year, Cambodia was still struggling to re-cover from genocide and extreme loss of lives. Every weekend, Phal and his younger brother placed a bucket of water aside the road. They would offered the water to the people who wandered through Phnom Penh to their hometowns and to rebuild their lives. There were thou-sands of people moving each day. Some were also looking for their families and relatives. When people stopped by for water, Phal would enquire them, "Where are you from? Do you know my relatives?" They would responded that they were from various places and they did not know Phal's relatives. Phal tried to ask people for many months. His persistence did not pay off.

Meeting Minister Hun Sen

Phal lived with Lork Ta Keo Chenda for three years. He always in-troduced Phal his civil servants in the ministry and other government officials. He also told people about the suffering Phal faced during the Khmer Rouge time and the loss of his parents, in particular being child survivors of S-21 along with his brother and two other children.

During the sixth anniversary of the establishment of the United Front for National Salvation of Kampuchea on 2 December 1984 which was held at the Royal Palace, Phal watched a film screening on white canvas in an open field in front of the palace. At that time, Prince Noro-dom Sihanouk had not yet returned to the country. That day Lork Ta Keo Chenda brought Phal to meet minister Hun Sen at his house near the Independence Monument. He told him Phal's family history. Min-ister Hun Sen immediately understood his plight having loss a new born son in the Khmer Rouge time himself. He gave Phal many pres-ents including new clothes, study materials, food and candies. With too much joy and still being a rough boy, Phal forgot to thank minister Hun Sen for his kindness. Lork Ta Keo Chenda had to bow down to instruct him the right way to return favor and respect for those who treat him nicely. Minister Hun Sen told Lork Ta Keo Chenda, "You keep the children at home. They cannot learn much since you are busy organizing the city. It is my advice that take them to an orphanage which our government has built to shelter lost children whose parents were killed by genocide and war. We have supplied food, shelters and educational materials there for a proper life for them. Teachers there can help them to grow as well as to learn."

Kolap Two Orphanage

Two months later, Lork Ta Keo Chenda decided to take Phal and his brother to Kolap Two Orphanage as advised by minister Hun Sen. The orphanage is currently Preah Ang Eng school in Phnom Penh. Phal was pleased and hopeful to be at the orphanage where he found many children of all ages already living there. The children were queuing in line with discipline. They looked at Phal with greeting gestures. Lork Ta Keo Chenda and teachers, then, stood in the middle of them and said, "Greeting all beloved nephews and nieces. We now have new members and they are child survivors of Tuol Sleng prison. You must take care of each other."

Meanwhile, the children gave a big round of applause as a sign of welcome to new members coming to live at the orphanage. After the meeting, children returned back to their respective classrooms. Lork

Ta Keo Chenda left after telling teachers and other children to look after Phal and his brother. Teachers showed Phal the room, class-rooms, and dining area. In the orphanage, teachers taught everyone to be well-disciplined, forgiving, looking after one another, sharing food and studying hard. For the daily routine at the orphanage, it was rise at 5 am, standing in line to do exercise at 6 am, gardening at 6:30 and going to the classroom 7 am. Lunch was prepared at 11 am. After three weeks at the orphanage, Phal realized that he was not the only ones who were separated from families and relatives. There were thousands of children at orphanages throughout the country. It was an enormous undertaking by the new government.

The government continued gathering parentless children from every village, district, and province. From months to months, the number of orphans kept increasing and resulted in insufficiency of materials such as study materials, clothes, shoes, and food. Life at the orphanage was getting hard but hopeful. During study and labor break, Phal left the orphanage with other children to pick up discarded vegetable and fruit at markets and harvest some inside the premises of the orphanage to take to the kitchen. The older children knew the environment outside the orphanage well. So they guided Phal to different parts of town. After a while Phal became familiar with the surroundings.

One day on a routine trip outside the orphanage to collect food, Phal ran across a familiar place. His team headed toward a place where there were many fruit trees. They knew this place and had visited it many times. As they arrived, those trees were empty. Other people had picked all the fruits. His team changed direction and headed south of the orphanage. As he traveled Phal started to recognize the road. He moved forward and saw tall barbed wire fences and metal gate. It was S-21. It was where the Khmer Rouge took his mother and him for imprisonment and torture. It was the place where by now Phal realized that his parents were taken to be brutally interrogated and executed.

Now that Phal was free to roam, Phal was both scared and excited to see it. He was scared because it used to control his life by a thread. He was excited and victorious because now it was no longer a powerful place any more. It was the subject of condemnation and symbolic of the Khmer Rouge's genocide. Phal told his friends to go inside to see it. They, however, had no courage to do so. They told Phal to get in by himself and they would wait outside. With last sight of his mother at the prison, Phal decided to walk in along and headed directly to the third building where the Khmer Rouge detained his mother. He found his mother's room remaining empty. The picture of her lying with him on the floor was, however, still vivid in his mind.

Meet Rui Kong, an S-21 Survivor

As Phal came out of the room, he caught a glimpse of a woman who was cleaning the building. Phal thought she was his mother and almost hugged her. She was just a cleaner. She asked Phal, "What are you doing here? What are you looking for?" Phal responded to her with tears, "I come here to look for my parents who the Khmer Rouge arrested from Kampong Speu to here. Do you know my mother? Have people ever looked for their children here?" She replied, "I do not know your mother and nobody ever looked for their children here. I am just a cleaner who came to work here for two months. I do not know much about what was going on here."

Seeing Phal cried, she told him, "You go downstairs to the second building and you'll see a grandfather whose name is Rui Kong. He is one of the seven victims who survived this prison. Maybe he knows more. You should go and ask him." Phal thanked her and walked downstairs as told to the second building. He turned to the left side and saw a 60-year-old skinny and seemingly weak man of around 168cm tall with grey hair, brown skin. He was clearing grass in the garden.

Phal stood behind him as he turned around. At that time, it seemed like he knew Phal. He suddenly dropped the hoe from his hand and touched Phal's head. He asked Phal, "Where do you live?" Phal replied, "I live at a nearby orphanage." Rui Kong continued, "Why do you come here?" Phal replied, "I come here because I want to hear news about my parents. Have people come here to look for their children?" He replied, "No, as I know, all prisoners who were detained here, were all murdered and there are only seven survivors. My family were all murdered here. Now, I live alone." After having a conversation for two hours, Rui Kong pulled his pocket, gave Phal 5 cents and said, "You should return to the orphanage. It is noon time. Your teachers might be looking for you. If anyone looks for their children, I will tell them about you."

Phal thanked the despairing old man and left. Some of Phal's friends had returned to the orphanage, only two waited for him. They rushed to get back to the orphanage and did not have time to talk. They returned late and had nothing for lunch. With the money that Rui Kong him, he was able to buy 10 pieces of rice cake to eat. At that moment, it became clearer to Phal that Toul Sleng was really a place where people were brought in to die and that the chance of reuniting with his parents became nonexistent. Since then, Rui Kong considered Phal as if he was his relative. In spare time, Phal took his younger brother to visit Toul Sleng prison which had been turned into a museum of genocide by the Cambodian government as evidence of Democratic Kampuchea's harsh treatment toward the Cambodian people.

Food Shortage

With more children being collected throughout the country without their parents, the orphanage became swollen with kids who were all in need of basic cares and education. Soon it became more difficult for the manager to fine enough food and other essentials to support the center. Phal's young younger brother always woke up in the middle of the night asking for his mother and food. Phal stole sugarcane from the orphanage's farm for his younger brother to make him stop crying a few times. However, with the missing sugarcanes, teachers started noticing. Phal tried another way to find food. Phal sneaked into the kitchen at night to see if there was any leftover. One time, he took a bag of liquid palm sugar weighing around half a kilogram. He took it too so that his brother would stop crying.

After drinking it with his brother, Phal thought about whether he should keep the remaining palm sugar or throw it away as far as possible to leave no trace. While he was thinking, a friend whose legs were crippled and was sleeping near him woke up. He asked Phal for it too. Phal thought it would be a waste if he threw the remaining liquid sugar palm away but if he gave it to his friend, it would be better. Phal gave it to him, told him to be careful and discard the bag away from everyone. His friend did not throw the bag far away. In the morning, the chef found it. The chef asked, "Did you eat the sugar?" At that time, Phal was terrified and afraid of getting blamed. He answered, "I don't know". The chef left but she suspected and asked Phal many times which Phal kept denying. The disabled child, who ate liquid sugar, had fever and was unable to go to class. A teacher asked why he had fever. The child confessed everything to the teacher. The next morning, the teacher asked Phal to hold a bag of sugar to show to all students and stand under sunlight. While he was being watched by other students, the teacher warned Phal to stop making mistakes from that day onward. Phal was embarrassed.

Every Khmer New Year, some elder people visited the orphanage and brought the children some food and fruit. Seeing what happened, his younger brother asked when his parents would visit him. Phal kept telling him that their parents would visit them one day. However, after living in the orphanage for a few years and making a lot of new friends, Norng Chan Ly stopped asking for his parents.

The shortage of food persisted. Phal and other children occasionally went out of the orphanage to food stores around the market. When people finished eating their rice or noodle soup, they poured remaining food into plastic bags, taking care not to break the plates to avoid being scolded away by the owners. Whenever there was a ceremony near the orphanage, Phal would help people do dishes. The organizers would feed him and give leftovers to take to the orphanage where he would feed his brothers and friends.

Phal and his friends soon learnt to take advantage of festivities. Every year, the Cambodian people always go to pagodas to offer food to monks in order to send their prayers to their ancestors who passed away in the Khmer Rouge regime and other reasons. For orphans like Phal who had no money or materials to offer to monks could only receive food from the pagodas. What most delighted about the 15 days of Pchum Ben was that his stomachs were filled for 15 days on end.

One day Phal's friends dressed nicely and put smiles on their faces. Phal tried asking them what they were up to. They said, "Join a wedding reception". Meanwhile, Phal thought that they were so honored to be invited to a wedding while Phal was not asked to go with them. He followed them to see what they were doing. When the sun set, he saw his friends went outside the orphanage one by one. There was indeed a wedding sight around 400 meters away from the orphanage. Maybe it was a wedding reception of children from well-off families. He continued observing. When guests left their tables, his friends collected remaining food to eat. Phal immediately copied their behavior and ate his fill.

After eating delicious wedding food, they separated and returned back to the orphanage one by one. Phal brought some food in a plastic bag for his brother and friends at the orphanage in the middle of the night. Some children, however, did not eat because they regarded it as waste. Those who ate had diarrhea the same night. After knowing the issue, teacher called Phal to a meeting and asked him to stand in the middle of 642 children. Then, he hit him with a cane stick three times and scolded him for not obeying discipline, going out to pick unclean food to share with other children, making those who obeyed discipline sick. It was a bad experience for him. He intended it to be a nice moment of sharing and abundance with his friends which turned out to be creating troubles for the teachers.

The discipline lesson from the teachers lowered Phal's status among his friends who started calling him "Toul Sleng prisoner." Other children stopped speaking much to him. His team membership in labor class, sports, agriculture and recreational activities were denied. Phal however could participate if teachers were nearby. Even his vegetable planting row was destroyed. A few children kicked a football into the face of Phal's younger brother who was playing nearby. His brother cried and Phal furiously questioned them for their behavior. One boy replied, "You, from Toul Sleng, also want to get hurt?" After hearing what he said and seeing his younger brother crying, Phal fought the boy. Only the teachers could separate them.

Survival Tricks

Cambodia and Vietnam were in good relations. Phal was always grateful for the Vietnamese and Cambodian soldiers who found and rescued him from S-21. Their care for him afterwards gave him hope and new belief in humanity. Emphasizing their care for the orphans, the two governments arranged for the orphans to conduct a study tour and participate in cultural exchange in Vietnam. Teachers selected and enlisted names of children who were intelligent and well-disciplined. After knowing the news, Phal rushed to check his names on the board but his and younger brother's names were not written on the list. To clarify, Phal went to ask his teacher why his name was not on the list. She explained that Phal made mistakes and did not obey the rules. To participate in the next tour, Phal must try to be a good student. Phal was disappointed after hearing those words but it was fair. On the departure day, Phal watched listed children waving goodbye.

Other children and Phal who had caused troubles were not allowed to go on a study tour to Vũng Tàu coastal town in Vietnam. Those remaining at the orphanage learnt their lessons. When there was any problem, they never pointed fingers at one another. Occasionally they snuck out together to find food and other fun activities without a cent in our pockets. When they queued to see a show, movie or game at the Olympic stadium, Phal noticed that his friends asked elder people to hold their hands and pretended like they were their children in order to get inside the stadium.

Some people were generous and allowed them to hold their hands while some were not. Phal followed what his friends did and he succeeded. He grinned a little when realizing the trick worked. As for a theater, when they got inside they needed to get into the restroom first; otherwise, without a seat allocation, they would be kicked out of it. Regardless of unpleasant smell in the restroom, they stayed there until the show started.

Reconciling with a Brother

On 18 August 1979, the government of the People's Republic of Kampuchea prosecuted senior Khmer Rouge leaders for killing three millions Cambodian people by establishing the People's Revolutionary Tribunal. Phal was chosen as a witness and provided a testimony to the court but it was incomplete since he was too young. After the country was liberated, many people were illiterate. Therefore, the ministry of education published books and publicized literacy program to the elders. In one of the books the ministry also included the backgrounds of child survivors who hid under a pile of clothes at S-21 under the topic: "Testimonial of Norng Chan Phal to the People's Revolutionary Tribunal".

In 1985, an old man living in Tram Kak district, Takeo province, read the literacy book and recognized the names of Norng Chen and Mom Yov. He knew that Phal's relatives were looking for him. He visited Chhouk district, Kampot province and handed the book to Phal's brother. He was excited to learn about Phal and his younger brother as he had been looking for his separated siblings for many years. He was poor and had little resources to search. He saved some money from selling his crops and logs. It took him seven months to save enough money to make the journey to meet Phal at the orphanage.

At that time, Cambodia had no taxis but there were trucks which transported food supply.Travelling by trucks was still expensive and dangerous due to congested riders. He, therefore, decided to come to Phnom Penh on foot. He spent three days walking to the city and he got lost with direction for other two days in the city. He asked tricycle drivers along the way until he found Kolap Two Orphanage which is now "Preah Ang Eng school". He went inside and asked teachers about Phal and his brother. A teacher then walked into Phal's classroom and asked, "Which one of you is Norng Chan Phal?" Phal quickly raised my hand in doubt. "There is a man from Kampot province looking for you. You should go to the playground and see if he is your relative," his teacher said. Hearing what his teacher said, Phal felt content and ran to the playground.

Phal tried to look around to see if there was any stranger but Phal saw only children playing balls and badminton. He stood still and saw a man, around 165cm tall, with dark skin covered with dirt. He stood in the middle of the crowd of children holding a small bag and conversing with them. The teacher approached Phal and asked, "Have you seen that man? Do you know him?" Phal answered, "Yes, teacher! I saw him but I do not know him." The teacher then called that man. He came closer, let go of his bag and hugged Phal. "Chan Phal! Chan Phal! Chan Phal!" The truth was that Phal separated from him ten years from 1976 to 1986. Phal could not recall his physical appearance but he could recognize his voice. His name was "Norng Chan Than". He narrated his story until Phal could not hold his tears. He asked Phal if their parents were dead or alive and where they were. Phal told him that their parents were murdered by the Khmer Rouge at S-21. Phal then asked for permission from the teacher to take his brother to Toul Sleng Genocide Museum and to seek for their parents' information.

The Death of Rui Kong

Upon arriving Toul Sleng Genocide Museum, Phal headed straight to Rui Kong to ask him information regarding their parents. He looked for him everywhere but he could not find him. Phal asked staff at the museum and learned that Rui Kong had died because of the internal injuries caused by the Khmer Rouge. After learning his death, Phal was deeply saddened because Rui Kong seemed like his only relative up until then. When returning to the orphanage, his brother made a request to the teacher to take Phal and his brother to live with him in Kampot. Phal wanted to leave the orphanage as soon as possible because he did not want to be called Toul Sleng prisoner. His brother's request was denied because Lork Ta Keo Chenda was the one who put Phal in the orphanage. The teacher could not make a decision.

Therefore, the teacher suggested his brother to seek for approval of Lork Ta Keo Chenda. In the next morning, we went to his house to seek his advice about my departure from the orphanage so that Phal could live with his brother in Kampot. Without thinking, Lork Ta Keo Chenda immediately denied the request and said, "You are poor. You cannot afford to send them to school. If you insist, you only take them to do farming with you or you can visit them when you miss them." Norng Chan Thorn thought over and decided to keep Phal and Norng Chan Ly at the orphanage. He returned to Kampot and promised to visit Phal every Khmer New Year and try to look for other relatives.

Change to New Orphanage

In 1986, the number of children in Kolab Two orphanage increased to an unsustainable level. With assistance from the Hungarian government, the Cambodian government was able to build a new orphanage in Kampong Kantuot village, Kandal Steung district, Kandal Province which was around 35 kilometers away from Phnom Penh on an area of 16 hectares. The complex consisted of many buildings and named "Hungarian Friendship Orphanage." Afterwards, children were allocated from other orphanages to live in the newly-built compound.

During the transfer, two orphans who were too young went missing. Phal and his brother were also transferred to the new orphanage. As soon as he stepped into the new place, he saw a pleasant landscape with beautiful garden with children playing at the playground and teachers smiling at new arrivals who were transferred from Phnom Penh. One of the teachers was a Hungarian national named Simon, who was 48 years old with white skin, a good height and a friendly smile. He then instructed children to go to inspect their new home.

For his past career, he was an air force doctor at Hungary. He volunteered to teach and provide medical treatment to children since he realized that they had poor health and that he could teach them some life skills including carpentry, blacksmithing, arts craft, agriculture and sports. This made Simon a popular figure among the children. They loved him as his father.

After staying at the orphanage for six months, the number of children increased dramatically leading to food shortage, drinking water shortage and lack of medicine. Some children had skin disease, fever, pneumonia and cough. Realizing the shortcomings of the orphanage, Simon returned to his country with reports to seek help. Phal and some children spent their spare time foraging outside the compound to catch fish and pick up fruits to eat. Phal walked far hoping to bring some fruits to his brother. Phal then reached a Jambolan plum tree (Pring tree) near a small stream outside the village, around six kilometers from the orphanage.

The tree trunk was not large enough for Phal to hold but he robustly climbed up the tree, feeling proud and strong as he did that. While he was focusing on picking the black fruits, he forgot about my own safety and what his friend advising me that the branch of this particular tree is easily broken. When climbing such a tree one needs to hold on to a larger branch. Phal tried to climb up to the top of the tree and the stem suddenly broke. Phal fell to the ground and fainted. Two hours later, Phal heard people chattering, "Jump over him for a couple times, he will regain consciousness." In Cambodian tradition, when someone meets an accident or faints, the one who witnesses it has to jump over him/her for three times before performing other emergency procedure. Phal opened his eyes and saw a pregnant woman jumping over him.

Phal could not speak so he raised his hand as a sign telling her to stop jumping. She, however, tripped over Phal and he fainted again. Twenty minutes later, Phal was conscious and shocked after learning that he fell from a ten meter tall tree with pain and injuries all over his body. The fall broke his left arm and shoulder blade and bleed his knee. A villager ran to inform teachers at the orphanage. Phal was sent to Lok Sang hospital (Kossamak hospital) in Phnom Penh but teachers did not stay long. They left Phal at the hospital and returned to the orphanage in the outskirt of town. Phal did not have money in his pocket or a caring relative. Phal was left at the hospital for three days without treatment and food. Phal was fortunate that other patients shared him their food. On day four, Simon returned from his country. When he arrived and heard that a child fell from a tree, he rushed to find Phal at the hospital. When he met Phal, he expressed his disappointment toward the hospital. He complained, "Why did the hospital and doctors leave a child without treatment for days? The wounds are not fresh and hard to be cured." He then took Phal back to the orphanage and performed a surgery on Phal by himself. After two months under a close care by Simon Phal fully recovered. Phal thanked him for his love and generosity.

Return to Orphanage in Phnom Penh

Later, another incident happened. A child named Chhun Haito fell from a palm tree and died. After the funeral, some children were fearful and fled the Hungarian Friend Orphanage to the orphanage in Phnom Penh. Realizing the differences between life in the city and in the countryside, my brother and I also fled to the orphanage in Phnom Penh. I sat for the grade 9 exam in 1990. The result was not as what I expected; I failed and I decided to quit school due to the lack of material and reaching mature age. I then found a mechanic school in Phnom Penh. That school, however, was not run by the state but private owners which required tuition fee. At that time, I started working at construction sites carrying materials.

Three months later, I saved some money and was about to register my name at that school. Fortunately, there was a civil society organization originated from France called Kary tas visited and distributed supply to the orphanage. Teachers requested the organization to provide tuition fee for me to study mechanical skills and welding at Khmer Dai Ek Technical School. After completing the course, I tried to find jobs at different automobile repair shops but I was unable to find one since most shops required 1 to 2 years of experience. Due to my short training time, I became a temporary staff to work everywhere for experience. I did not earn good sum of money. However, there were more works to do compared to automobile repair shops. For me, I accepted my payment no matter how high or low. I needed experience and knowledge only.

Orphans Receiving Hungarian Delegates in 1986[42]

---

42 *Photo courtesy of CIPD.*

Orphans Receiving Hungarian Delegates in 1986

Norng Chan Phal in 1987 (Left)[43]

5. TRUTH SEEKING, JUSTICE AND CLOSURE

On 23 October 1993, the Kingdom of Cambodia changed its regime from socialism to democracy. The Cambodian people and factions re-united and repatriated back to the country. Phal was able to meet two sisters and one brother. His eldest sister died in 1979 during evacuation.

On 27 April 1994, since he had knowledge on how to operate and maintain trucks, the World Family recruited him providing modest salary to support his living condition. Phal gave some of the money to his youngest brother for schooling. World Family was an organization dedicated to conserving the environment. They sent Phal to Bali, Indonesia, to learn about advantages of bamboo trees which could be used in the construction sector and other fields without the need to use woods. This training was like a rendezvous for Phal as his father was a carpenter in the 1960s. He attended the course for three months and learned how to make beds, closets, tables, furniture, and souvenir made from bamboo trees. After completing the course, he shared what he learned with other Cambodians to let them understand advantages of bamboo trees. Phal returned with a sense of pride for abundance of natural resources of his home country, Cambodia. He said, "These activities made me feel so proud of my own nation."

In 1995, Phal met a woman when he was on his mission to Sihanouk Ville and started a relationship with her. He told her that he was an orphan whose parents were both killed by the Khmer Rouge. However, Phal did not tell her about his past at Tuol Sleng because he was afraid that it would affect her feeling. The two were soon engaged. A few months later they married with participation and blessing of Mr. Daniel Soshot, director of the World Family, and other elders who were his neighbors. Two years later, World Family shut down due to lack of funding.

After the closure, Phal was unemployed for three months. One day, his wife's friend visited them and asked his wife why she got married with Phal who was unemployed, poor, and parentless. Hearing those words, Phal was devastated. His wife responded to her friend that she was in love with him because I was an orphan who was helpful and hard working. Those words spoken by his wife gave him motivation to find work and work even harder.

Not long afterwards, Phal learned how to drive bulldozer and excavator for two months from those who had experience. He then handled a brand-new bulldozer. He was very delighted since he could earn money to support his family. Later on, his younger brother, Norng Chan Ly, became a part of the team and drove sand truck. Under his new responsibility Phal felt proud and said, "My brother, our co-workers, and I were satisfied with our work since Cambodia was torn by wars for many decades; bridges, dams, buildings, irrigation system, and infrastructure were severely destructed. On behalf of a Cambodian citizen, I had to share my responsibility to reconstruct what was destroyed. I had built numerous roads in many provinces and cities."

Revisit Khmer Rouge Village

In 1998, his construction team was assigned a project to build a road in Treng Trayeung commune, Phnom Srouch District, Kampong Speu Province, where he used to live during the Khmer Rouge regime with his parents and relatives. Phal went to a hut located in a thick forest and sat there. As he swept leaves on the ground, he found a spoon which his mother used to eat porridge while she was sick. He walked into a village and asked about the background of this village in the past 20 years. People were afraid to tell him everything they knew because he was a stranger and they were concerned that he might bring trouble to them.

One morning, while he was driving a bulldozer, he saw a 60-year-old man whom he knew riding a bicycle with vegetable. "Where are you taking vegetable to?" Phal asked. "I take it to sell at Treng Trayeung Market," he answered. Heaing that Phal helped buying his vegetable to establish a friendly relationship with him. He then told Phal his name was Mao and that he was a former village chief and staff of the workshop of Phal's father. Mao reported that a week after the Khmer Rouge arrested Norng Chen, they shot Norng Chreuk who was Phal's uncle in front of the workshop witnessed by other workers. Phal continued for some unknown reasons, "To dig up grass, the Khmer Rouge had to remove even the roots." Mao added that he knew the offenders' names. But they had all moved away several years before.

Justice, Reconciliation and Healing

Today Phal is a happy family man bearing no grudge against the Khmer Rouge. He has worked hard to transition from orphans to a father and a husband. The only thing in his mind is justice for the death of his parents during the final days of the genocide. Phal never resisted opportunity to meet former Khmer Rouge officials. He met often S-21 guard named Him Huy but the two have gone well together. In his own words, Phal said, "The Cambodian people and I survived the injustice, tragedy, murder of innocent people during the Khmer Rouge regime. When the Khmer Rouge tribunal prosecutes senior Khmer Rouge officials most responsible for the reprehensible crimes, I felt delighted. I learnt about this tribunal in 2007. After I heard that Kaing Guek Eav, aka Duch, former chief of S-21was arrested and brought to the tribunal, I was overjoyed and hoped that the Court would find justice for my family and the Cambodian people." On 3 February 2012, Kaing Guek Eav was sentenced to life imprisonment by the ECCC[44] on the crime against humanity and grave breaches of the 1949 Geneva conventions. Upon hearing the news, Phal said, "I am very happy because the deaths of my parents have been made a decision concerning a law-

---

44 See ECCC's Case 001 Appeal Judgment at https://www.eccc.gov.kh/en/document/court/case-001-appeal-judgement

suit. I am very happy that the court has found justice for me and my parents. This is what I want".[45]

Today Phal is no longer ashamed about being a prisoner at the notorious Khmer Rouge security office. He openly talks about it and wants the world to know his story and millions other miseries of the Cambodian people suffering under the hand of the radical leaders. Indeed, Phal provided testimony to the Khmer Rouge tribunal and is currently working at Toul Sleng Genocide Museum. A museum visitor told him to keep going, "You have to talk about what you have been through and compile it as documents for the younger generations to learn and share. When you unfold your story to other people, you will feel relieved." That is exactly Phal did when he participated in the Khmer Rouge tribunal. He said:

> "Filing a complaint and providing a testimonial against Duch at the ECCC attracted so much attention from the international community. They could not believe that there were child survivors at Tuol Sleng Prison. Duch's defense team denied that there was no child survivor at the Prison and that everything was set up by the Vietnamese. I was furious. I believe that Duch is still remorseless. When Duch later saw the biographies of my parents from the Tuol Sleng Prison Duch admitted that my parents were among the last ones to be taken in. Do you believe that Duch is remorseful?"

The Spoon Norng Chan Phal Found in His Mother Cottage

45 ECCC VSS Newsletter, Vol. 2 Issue No. 07: April – June 2012. P.2.

Norng Chan Phal's Marriage in 1995

FORGIVENESS AFTER KHMER ROUGE GENOCIDE
Kok-Thay ENG
14 October 2010

I am delighted that on 15 September 2010, the Extraordinary Chambers in the Courts of Cambodia announced that the four remaining senior Khmer Rouge leaders currently in custody – Nuon Chea, Ieng Sary, Khieu Samphan and Ieng Thirith – were indicted for crimes against humanity and genocide, among other offenses.

I hope that they will be tried fairly and punished justly according to the law. What they did to the people of Cambodia was beyond hell on earth. They were the devil of humanity. But can they be forgiven by the people? The four accused invited monks to their cells to preside over an offering ceremony during the Pchum Ben holiday. This is an indication that they might be seeking forgiveness for their next lives or somebody to take care of them when they die.

On Pchum Ben people send food to bret (lost souls or wandering ghosts) who have committed serious sins during their lifetimes and cannot be reborn. The enormity of the crimes committed by leaders of the Khmer Rouge could make them the worst bret of all, who would always be hungry and wandering without destination. If they can be forgiven by survivors, their prospect for life after death could be improved.

Forgiveness does not call for release or dissolution of the ECCC. Forgiveness is a very sensitive question. It is almost a taboo to ask victims or the public to consider. But I would like them to try. Complete justice after genocide is never possible. Without such justice, people are forced to live with a sense of injustice, grudges, anger and frustration. Those mental conditions negatively affect survivors to such an extent that without measures to cope, they can destroy them from inside.

Much like the Khmer Rouge's own oft-cited slogan that the most contemptible of enemies are those "burrowing from within" and must be rooted out immediately, the atrocities of the Khmer Rouge genocide created mental conditions that have been burrowing inside survivors, for some people causing acute cases of mental disorder. On the other hand, whether admitting it or not, some people have been able to forgive the perpetrators.

During the Duch verdict announcement, I visited a remote village in Kampong Thom province in which Pin, a former Khmer Rouge and perpetrator, and Pai, a survivor, have lived together for almost 30 years. Pin was involved in killing Pai's one-legged husband in 1977. Although Pin never admitted that he killed Pai's husband, simultaneous interviews with both of them revealed the chilling story of how Pai's husband died.

On a cloudless afternoon in Kampong Thom, Pin and his comrade walked up to Pai's house, tied her husband to its central column, interrogated him for a short time and then took him into the bush not far away from the village. Pin said Pai's husband did not resist. He and his comrade escorted him to the bush with a hoe, and he knew full well that the hoe would be used as an execution tool. Pin said Pai's husband's hands were tied behind him fairly loosely, but that he did not attempt to escape.

Arriving at the bush, Pai's husband was made to sit down and struck with the hoe. Pin did not describe clearly how Pai's husband was killed, he just said, "My comrade did the job." In the early 1980s, Pai excavated a shallow grave and found a one-legged skeleton with broken arms and fractured skull. Pin never said anything about the manner of his death, but judging from the trauma on the skeleton, Pai's husband died a brutal death.

Pin's comrade who supposedly committed the act died many years ago. Pai witnessed Pin killing another person in the village. She saw how cold-blooded he was when taking a rifle and shooting the man like "a raging dog in full daylight". Today Pin is living with his wife and two children. During the day he works in a pagoda to help the monks. He is old and frail. Pai's four children have grown up. Two of them are able-bodied men.

Overall, the family is much better off than Pin's, meaning they could physically take revenge on Pin and few people in the village would consider it to be an injustice, or they could use their better social status to make Pin's life much worse than it already is. But Pai said, "I don't want to kill him, and I have stopped my children from doing so. I want him to live so that he can take care of his wife and children."

Pai does not want to see another woman become a widow and go through her same experience.

Pai said that Pin is being punished by the Buddha for what he did. His mental capacity is weak, and he is virtually an outcast in the village. Only the pagoda provides a haven for him.

Even though Pai never talks about forgiveness, in many respects she has forgiven Pin and has moved on with her life. Pai does not have to love Pin to forgive him. She does not have to communicate with him to forgive him. To Pai, Pin is a sad case of Buddha's example of living sin, to be rejected forever by survivors, society and his own self.

Anyone falling into this category should be pitied. Perhaps one day, Pin will realise that the only way to rid himself of his sin is to continue collecting merits from the pagoda and repay Pai anyway possible. When that happens, a complete forgiveness and reconciliation may be possible.

If Pin chooses the easy way by denying his crime, then complete forgiveness is not possible.

For Pai, denial from Pin does not affect her, but admission increases her sense of enlightenment.

I believe this example is being lived in many other locations in Cambodia. People do not want to admit that it is happening because they would be seen as weak and surrendering to the perpetrators. Forgiveness is a very personal matter. The path varies from person to person. It depends on how much harm was done, the demeanor of the perpetrators and the life philosophy of survivors. It is possible for one to forgive entirely by oneself without interaction with the perpetrators. Also, forgiveness does not mean abandoning legal accountability. Forgiveness can be taught if one sees enough successful examples. However, forgiving the four Khmer Rouge leaders is a different story. Will the devil of humanity be forgiven? Will Case 002 lay such a foundation for Cambodians in general to move beyond grudges? It will be a difficult test for forgiveness and reconciliation in Cambodia.

BIBLIOGRAPHY

Ben Kiernan and Chanthou Boua, *Peasants and Politics in Kampuchea, 1942-1981,* London: Zed Press, 1982.

Ben Kiernan, (2nd Ed.), *How Pol Pot Came to Power: Colonialism, Nationalism, and Communism in Cambodia, 1930-1975,* New Haven & London: Yale University Press, 2004.

Ben Kiernan, (ed.), *Genocide and Democracy in Cambodia: The Khmer Rouge, the United Nations and the International Community,* New Haven: Yale University Southeast Asia Studies, 1993.

Benny Widyono, *Dancing in Shadows: Sihanouk, The Khmer Rouge, and the United Nations in Cambodia,* New York: Rowman & Littlefield Publishers, INC., 2008.

Caroline Hughes, *The Political Economy of Cambodia's Transition: 1991-2001,* London and New York: RoutledgeCurzon, 2003.

Charles Higham, *The Civilization of Angkor,* Berkeley and Los Angeles: University of California Press, 2002.

David Ayres, *Anatomy of a Crisis: Education, Development, and the State in Cambodia 1953-1998,* Honolulu: University of Hawaii Press, 2000.

David Chandler, (3rd Ed.), *A History of Cambodia,* Boulder: Westview Press, 2000.

David Chandler, (Rev. Ed.), *Brother Number One: A Political Biography of Pol Pot,* Boulder: Westview Press, 1999.

David Chandler, Ben Kiernan, and Chanthou Boua, (Transl. and Eds.),

Pol Pot Plans the Future: Confidential Leadership Documents from Democratic Kampuchea, 1976-1977, New Haven: Yale University Southeast Asia Studies, 1988.

Evan Gottesman, *Cambodia after the Khmer Rouge: Inside the Politics of Nation Building,* New Haven and London, Yale University Press, 2003.

Francois Bizot, (Transl.), *The Gate,* New York: Alfred Knopf, 2003.

Frank Stewart and Sharon May, (eds.), *In the Shadow of Angkor: Contemporary Writing from Cambodia,* Hawaii: University of Hawaii Press, 2004.

Haing Ngor, *Survival in the Killing Fields,* New York: Carroll & Graf Publishers, 2003.

Heather Clark, *When There Was No Money: Building ACLEDA Bank in Cambodia's Evolving Financial Sector,* New York: Springer, 2006.

Helene Cixous, (Transl.), *The Terrible but Unfinished Story of Norodom Sihanouk, King of Cambodia,* Lincoln and London: University of Nebraska Press, 1994.

Henry Kamm, *Cambodia: Report from a Stricken Land,* New York: Arcade Publishing, 1998.

Howard De Nike, John Quigley, and Kenneth Robinson, (eds.), *Genocide in Cambodia: Documents from the Trial of Pol Pot and Iang Sary,* Philadelphia: University of Pennsylvania Press, 2000.

Ian Mabbett and David Chandler, *The Khmers,* Oxford UK & Cambridge USA: Blackwell, 1995

Jan Myrdal and Gunkessle, (Translated from Swedish by Paul Britten

Austin), *Angkor: An Essay on Art and Imperialism,* New York: Pantheon Books, 1970.

John Armstrong, *Sihanouk Speaks,* New York: Walker and Company, 1964

John Tully, *A Short History of Cambodia: From Empire to Survival,* Australia: Allen & Unwin, 2005.

Judy Ledgerwood, (ed.), *Cambodia Emerges from the Past: Eight Essays,* Dekalb: Southeast Asia Publications, 2002.

Julie Canniff, *Cambodian Refugees' Pathway to Success: Developing a Bi-Cultural Identity,* New York: LFB Scholarly Publishing, 2001.

Karen Coates, *Cambodia Now: Life in the Wake of War,* North Carolina: McFarland & Company, 2005.

Kathryn Robson and Jennifer Yee, (eds.), *France and "Indochina": Cultural Representations,* New York: Lexington Books, 2005.

Kiernan, Ben, (2nd ed.), *The Pol Pot Regime: Race, Power, and Genocide in Cambodia under the Khmer Rouge, 1975-1979,* New Haven and London: Yale University Press, 2002.

Manich Jumsal, *History of Thailand and Cambodia: From the Days of Angkor to the Present,* Bangkok: Chalermnit, 1970.

Margaret Slocomb, *The People's Republic of Kampuchea 1979-1989: The Revolution after Pol Pot,* Chiang Mai: Silkworm Books, 2003.

May Ebihara, Carol Mortland & Judy Ledgerwood, (eds.), *Cambodian Culture Since 1975: Homeland and Exile,* Ithaca and London: Cornell University Press, 1994.

Michael Freeman, *Cambodia,* London: Reakton Books, 2004.

Milton Obsorne, *Before Kampuchea: Preludes to Tragedy,* London: George Allen & Unwin, 1984

Milton Osborne, (9th Ed.), *Southeast Asia: An Introductory History,* NSW Australia: Allen & Unwin, 2004.

Milton Osborne, *Politics and Power in Cambodia: The Sihanouk Years,* Australia: Longman Australia, 1973.

Milton Osborne, *Sihanouk: Prince of Light, Prince of Darkness,* Honolulu: University of Hawaii Press, 1994.

Milton Osborne, *Southeast Asia: An Illustrated Introductory History,* Sydney: George Allen & Unwin, 1985.

Milton Osborne, *The French Presence in Cochinchina and Cambodia: Rule and Response (1859-1905),* Ithaca and London: Cornell University Press, 1969.

Milton Osborne, *The Mekong: Turbulent Past,* Uncertain Future, New York: Atlantic Monthly Press, 2000.

Penny Edwards, *Cambodge: The Cultivation of a Nation, 1860-1945,* Honolulu: University of Hawaii Press, 2007.

Peter Maguire, *Facing Death in Cambodia,* New York: Columbia University Press, 2005.

Philip Short, Pol Pot: *Anatomy of a Nightmare,* New York: Henry Holt and Company, 2005.

Susan Cook, (ed.), *Genocide in Cambodia and Rwanda: New Perspectives*, New Brunswick: Transaction Publishers, 2005.

Tom Fawthrop and Helen Javis, *Getting Away with Genocide?: Elusive Justice and the Khmer Rouge Tribunal*, London: Pluto Press, 2004.

Vann Nath, (Transl.), A Cambodian Prison Portrait: One Year in the Khmer Rouge's S-21, Bangkok: White Lotus Press, 1998.

Wilfred Burchett, *The Second Indochina War: Cambodia and Laos*, New York: International Publishers, 1970.

William Logan, (ed.), *The Disappearing "Asian" City: Protecting Asia's Urban Heritage in a Globalizing World*, Oxford: Oxford University Press, 2002.

William Shawcross, *Sideshow: Kissinger, Nixon, and the Destruction of Cambodia*, New York: Cooper Square Press, 2002.

William Shawcross, The Quality of Mercy: Cambodia, Holocaust and Modern Conscience, New York: Simon and Schuster, 1984.

ARCHIVAL MATERIALS

DC-Cam Document D00049: Biography of Comrade Tiv Ol aka Penh

DC-Cam Document D00480: Study the Four-Year Plan.

DC-Cam Document D07309: The Confession of Hou Nim aka Phoas.

DC-Cam Document D07396: Confession of Chan Sarat.

DC-Cam Document D13840: The Case of Penh Thuok aka Sok or Vorn Vet, Minister of Industry.

DC-Cam Document D15143: Koy Thuon aka Khuon's Brief Activities.

DC-Cam Document D15572: Koy Thuon aka Khuon's Background and Activities.

DC-Cam Document D21281: Confession of Moul Oun aka Moul Sambath, June 14, 1978. [Ros Nhim].

DC-Cam Document D21642: National Constitution of Democratic Kampuchea.

DC-Cam Document D23250: The Activities of the Traitor, Koy Thuon.

DC-Cam Document D38615: Politburo Profiles, October 1985.

DC-Cam Document J00404: Confession of Tan Try aka Chhoeun.

DC-Cam Document J00410: Confession of Chin Ear aka Sou.

DC-Cam Document J00502: Traitorous Activities of Tiv Ol aka Penh.

DC-Cam Document J00610: Confessions of Lao Sros.

DC-Cam Document L1045: Telegram 15.

DC-Cam Document L1449: Minutes of Meeting between Secretaries and Deputy Secretaries of Divisions and Regiments.

DC-Cam Document: Khmer Rouge Liberated Zone May 1972.

DC-Cam Document: Khmer Rouge Liberated Zone May 1973.

DC-Cam Document: *Revolutionary Youth Magazine,* August 1974.

DC-Cam Document: *Revolutionary Youth Magazine,* February 1974.

DC-Cam Document: *Revolutionary Youth Magazine,* July 1975.

DC-Cam Document: Map of Democratic Kampuchea 1976.

AUTHOR'S INTERVIEWS

Author's interview with Chea Im, 1 July 2012
Author's interview with Chea Phal, 30 June 2012
Author's interview with Hiem Khoeun, 30 June 2012
Author's interview with Lorng Lao, 28 June 2012
Author's interview with Meas Pov, 10 June 2012
Author's interview with Nhek Seun, 5 June 2012
Author's interview with Nou Naom, 2 July 2012
Author's interview with Sim Than, 2 July 2012
Author's interview with Sok Khan, 3 July 2012
Author's interview with Soun Thy, 27 June 2012
Author's interview with Yeay Kiek, 27 June 2012
Author's interview with Yoeung Oeun, 11 June 2012
Author's interview with Aun Long, 1 March 2018
Author's interview with Kae Mat, M, November 24, 2011.
Author's interview with Keo Ibrohim, M, 63, October 2, 2011.
Author's interview with Li Chib, F, 70, March 24, 2012.
Author's interview with Loh Mae, M, November 24, 2010.
Author's interview with Ly Mat, M, August 26, 2010.
Author's interview with Mae You, M, January 29, 2011.
Author's interview with Neak Manan, F, September 18, 2010.
Author's interview with No Sreinob, August 26, 2010.